The Gorgeless Gourmet's
COOKBOOK

Mrs. Clarice Plog,
    Hope this gets you out
of the kitchen fast!
        Ferris Robinson

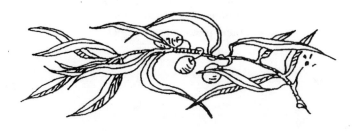

by
Ferris Kelly Robinson

Illustrations by Mary Ferris Kelly

Ferris Robinson publishes The Gorgeless Gourmet - the practically
fat-free newsletter for super-busy people. Her recipes have
been pictured and featured in Woman's World magazine.
She regularly writes food columns for Senior Magazine,
The Chattanooga News Free Press, and other periodicals.

Peach Publishing
Box 366
Lookout Mountain, TN 37350
(706) 820-4169

First printing October 1996
Second printing November 1996
Third printing January 1997
Fourth printing March 1997

For Dan Robinson,
the best man I know.

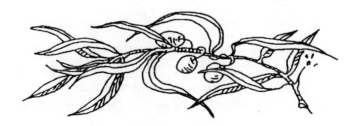

Acknowledgments

I don't know if I ever would have written this cookbook if it hadn't been for the letters I've received from people suggesting the use of such a book. I *know* I wouldn't have put the fat grams, calories and nutritional values in this book if it weren't for readers strongly requesting this information.

Thanks to my brother, Buzz Kelly, and Angie Moore for insisting that I include the nutritional values when I tried to weasel out of it. I painstakingly calculated the data reluctantly, cursing them all the way. However, due to their bullheadedness and to my computer and to Kelly Robinson, the values are included.

I appreciate the folks at the Lookout Mountain Post Office for making what could be a tedious part of my job such a pleasure.

I'd also like to thank my sister, Woo Kelley, for hauling her brood up to my house to help me when I was desperate and my mother, for dropping everything to do the artwork for this book. And I will always remember with a twinge in my heart the pages of my first cookbook that my father helped me collate many years ago in the basement.

Finally I would like to thank my sons, Alex, Robby and Mikey, for tasting everything on these pages and for tolerating my obsession with this book. And my husband's unfailing encouragement means the world. Thank you all.

INTRODUCTION

I never set out to write a low-fat cookbook. In fact,
I learned to cook with rouxs and cheese sauces and
Half & Half. I didn't think food could taste like
anything worth eating without a lot of fat, but
didn't give it much thought, period, because, well,
because there was really no reason to put ourselves
through what I thought of as deprivation.

When my husband had open-heart surgery at the
age of 34, everything changed. The surgeon told us
Dan would drastically have to change his lifestyle,
meaning diet, exercise and stress, and I knew I
couldn't do much about exercise and stress (besides
screaming at him less), but I knew I could help with
his diet.

I spent the first few weeks poring over cookbooks
and adding serious mileage to my odometer by
scouring the city for lemon grass and tahini and
other things I'd never heard of, much less bought. I
piled my sink high with sauté pans, holding pans,
roasting pans and braising pans, and that was just
for one dish.

It didn't take long for me to figure out this new

system of fat-free cooking wasn't going to work at my house. I was resentful, my boys were disgruntled and the food was terrible. After what seemed like an endless number of quick and easy fat-free experiments the dog wouldn't eat, I finally made a dish the bunch of them wolfed down. Then I made another and another and before I knew it, friends who didn't give a flip about cholesterol or fat began calling for my recipes because they were downright *good*!

My friend Erin Chapin suggested I write a newsletter, and <u>The Gorgeless Gourmet - practically fat-free recipes for super-busy people</u>, was born.

This cookbook came about for two basic reasons. First of all, I had many more requests for back issues of my newsletter than I had newsletters, and secondly, I got sick and tired of searching through 22 newsletters for a recipe I needed! I figured if I wrote the newsletters and still couldn't find a recipe, there must be hundreds of people out there cursing me at meal times when they couldn't remember if Santa Fe Chicken Ole was in the March issue or the May issue— and I get enough cursing at home around dinnertime (i.e., hell hour).

At any rate, here are the best of almost two years of the Gorgeless Gourmet in an organized format. I hope you enjoy these recipes, and that you get out of the kitchen fast!

Table Of Contents

Fat-Free Pantry   9
Menus   11
Appetizers   13
Salads   23
Soups   41
Vegetables   57
Main Dishes   91
Pasta   135
Desserts   157
Miscellaneous   181

Note: If the vitamins in a recipe were above 10% of the daily requirement, I included them in the nutritional data. Otherwise, I just listed calories, fat, sodium, carbohydrates and proteins.

FAT-FREE PANTRY

Or Things I Can't Do Without

Nonstick Skillet with Lid - My mother presented me with a really good nonstick skillet after Dan's heart surgery, and I have worn it out. I can throw in a mess of vegetables with a little wine or tomato juice or fat-free salad dressing or chicken broth, cover it and saute without oil!

Naturally Fresh Balsamic Vinaigrette - Fat-free and so good you won't believe it. I use it for marinades, sauteeing and tossing with pasta. Look in refrigerated dressing section in grocery store. Delicious! (404-765-9000 in Atlanta — It's worth tracking down.)

Walden Farm Sun-Dried Tomato Dressing - Fat-free and wonderful!

T.Marzetti's Spinach Salad Dressing - Fat-free and so good heated up and tossed with fresh spinach, Mandarin oranges and red onion slices.

Marie's Blue Cheese Dressing - 7 grams of fat for 2 tablespoons, but mix it with **7-Seas Red Wine Oil and Vinegar Dressing** for a fabulous, low fat dressing.

Louis Rich Turkey Bacon - The white part is actually turkey breast and the dark part the thigh. My kids actually prefer it over real bacon.

Loius Rich Turkey Kielbasa Sausage - I try to keep a pack in my freezer for bean soups, beans and rice, etc.

Overbrook Farms Chicken & Pasta - Speaking of the freezer, this is a staple. You can't beat it for those rushed afternoons when dinner is the last thing on your mind. (2.5 grams of fat for 1 cup. At Sam's Wholesale Warehouse)

Healthy Choice Breakfast Sausage - 1.5 grams of fat for 2 patties. My husband loves these in one of Elise's Biscuits.

Light Velveeta Cheese - Creamy and luscious, this is great in casseroles and melted on sandwiches and just about everywhere!

Creamy Potato Soup by J&M Marketing - You only add water to this dry soup mix and it is outstanding! They mail order out of Nashville, TN. (615-383-5864)

Low Fat Moon Pies - Try heating one of these up and enjoying it with a glass of skim milk. (800-251-3404)

Healthy Choice Pop Corn - 2 1/2 grams of fat per serving and has the best taste for the amount of fat I've found.

Healthy Choice Cappuccino Chocolate Chunk Ice Cream - 2 grams of fat for 1/2 cup and is totally delicious.

Healthy Choice Mint Chocolate Chip Ice Cream - You won't miss the fat-filled variety with this.

Guilt Free Sour Cream - the best fat-free sour cream around.

Guilt Free Egg Nog - really, really good.

Kellogs Low-Fat Pop Tarts - 3 grams of fat each. Spread a little fat-free butter on one and pop it under the broiler and settle down with a big cold galass of skim milk and watch a rerun of Lassie. You'll forget you're a day over 12.

Downey's Honey Butter - 1 gram of fat per tablespoon. Spread it over a bagel, toast it and enjoy!

Fleischmann's Fat-Free Margarine - this comes in a squeeze bottle and is good and so easy to use.

Fat-Free Cool Whip - Thank Goodness.

Cavender's Greek Seasoning - this is with the spices and has about half the sodium of salt and a great flavor. I use it on just about everything.

Cilantro - This is with the fresh parsley in the produce section and adds a wonderful Mexican flavor.

MENUS

<u>One Pot Meals</u>

Santa Fe Chicken Ole
Add orange wedges and French bread.

Poulet in a Pot
French bread is all you need.

Tomato Sage Chicken
French bread makes this a meal.

Potato Crusted Chicken
Green salad

All Lasagnas
Big green salad & French bread

All Soups
Crusty bread

<u>Dinner When Lesser People Would Have Picked Up McDonalds'</u>

Pasta in a Panic

Angie's Red Beans & Rice

Katie's Black Bean Soup

Monkey Hips & Rice

Dinner When You're Not Home To Cook

Poulet in a Pot
(You've got about 2 hours to go to the mall, get a pedicure, or more likely, drive carpool.)

Tomato-Sage Chicken
(Take the afternoon off.)

Crock Pot Chicken
(You've got a good hour here.)

All the Lasagnas (There's no need to cook the noodles. You can also make the lasagna the day before and refrigerate it until it's time to cook it.)

Company's Coming

Stuffed Chicken Breasts
Fruited Wild Rice
Buckhead Spinach Salad

Pearl's Pork Tenderloin
Garlic Mashed Potatoes
Spring Veggies

Pork Tenderloins with Apricot Glaze
Fruited Wild Rice
Broccoli Red Pepper Salad

Spinach Calzones

Appetizers

Bueno Bites

I made these and they were gone faster than Speedy Gonzoles!

4 large fat-free flour tortillas
1 8-oz. pkg. fat free cream cheese (Philadelphia)
1/2 cup salsa
1/4 cup fresh cilantro
1/2 cup fat-free cheddar cheese

Mix cream cheese, salsa and cilantro, and spread on tortillas. Sprinkle with cheddar cheese, then roll up. Refrigerate a couple of hours, then slice into bite-size pieces. Serves 4-6 at 0 fat grams.

Joanie's Sausage Dip

This is hearty, cheesy and spicy!

1 (6.4 oz.) pkg. Healthy Choice Sausage Patties
1 (8-oz.) block fat-free cream cheese
4 oz. light Velveeta Cheese
1 can Rotel tomatoes

In nonstick skillet, crumble sausage patties and brown. Add cream cheese and heat until cheese melts. Add Velveeta and tomatoes and stir until melted. Serve immediately with fat-free tortilla chips.

Serves 10 - 12 at 2 fat grams per serving. Other nutritional data not available.

Manly Tex-Mex

This is easy and packed with nutrition!

1 8-oz. block fat-free cream cheese, softened
1 bottle Picante sauce
1 can black beans, drained
1 t. minced garlic
1/2 cup chopped red or yellow pepper
1/4 cup chopped green onion
fat-free sour cream

Mix cream cheese with Picante sauce. Mix beans with remaining vegetables. In shallow bowl, layer bean mixture, then Picante mixture then top with dollops of sour cream and fresh cilantro. Serve with low-fat tortilla chips.

Serves 6 at 1 fat gram and 222 calories per serving. 45% A, 47% C, 19% calcium, 322 mg. sodium, 29 g. carb., 14 g. protein

Fiery Bean Dip

This is as easy as it is good.

1 (16-oz.) can fat-free refried beans
4 oz. light Velveeta cheese, cubed
1 cup chunky salsa
1 T. fresh cilantro, chopped
1 T. chopped green onions

Mix beans, cheese and salsa together in microwave-safe bowl, then cook for about 5 minutes, until cheese is melted. Garnish with cilantro and green onions and serve with low-fat tortilla chips. Serves 8 at less than 2 fat grams per serving.

Pure Texas

This is a real man-pleaser.

1 (16-oz.) can fat-free refried beans
1 (8-oz.) carton fat-free sour cream
1 packet (1.25 oz.) taco seasoning
1 large tomato, chopped
1 bunch green onions, chopped
1 cup fat-free shredded cheddar cheese
1 cup chunky salsa
2 T. chopped fresh cilantro

Spread beans in quiche pan or shallow serving dish. Mix sour cream and taco seasoning and spread over beans. Layer tomato, onions, cheese, salsa and sprinkle cilantro over top. Serve with low-fat tortilla chips. Serves about 12 at 0 fat grams.

Sherried Cream Cheese Dip with Chutney

This is both elegant and easy!

2 (8-oz) blocks fat-free cream cheese
1/4 t. curry
1 T. sherry
1 t. garlic salt
1 T. parsley
1 bottle Major Gray's Mango chutney (usually with relishes in grocery)
1 bunch green onions, chopped

Mix cream cheese, curry, sherry, garlic salt, and parsley with mixer. Spread in quiche pan or shallow round dish and top with chutney, then sprinkle with onions. Serve with fat-free wheat crackers. (Snackwell's Wheat Crackers are good)

Serves about 10 at 0 fat grams and 69 calories per serving. 134 mg. sodium, 16 g. carb., 2 g. protein

Hummus

This is as easy as it can be, and delicious to boot.

1 can garbanzo beans, drained
2 cloves garlic,minced (or 1 t. from jar)
2 T. lemon juice
1/2 red pepper, chopped
4 rounds whole wheat Pita bread

Put beans, garlic and lemon juice in blender. Whirl until semi-blended. Add red pepper and whirl until definitely blended, but the pepper is not pureed. Cut edges of bread with scissors (making 2 circles from each round) and toast. When toasted, cut into triangles and serve with hummus.

Party Pizzas

These make yummy appetizers, and can also be made for individual dinner pizzas.

1 loaf frozen bread dough
2 -3 sliced tomatoes
2 Vidalia onions, sauteed in H2O
basil
garlic
 Fat free Parmesan cheese

Thaw bread according to directions. Roll into 5 small, circles with rolling pin. Brush with garlic and sprinkle with basil and Parmesan. Layer each with onion and tomato and sprinkle with more Parmesan. Bake at 375 for 20 minutes or until crust is done.

Makes 5 little pizzas at 4 fat grams per pizza and 45 calories per slice (4 slices per pizza) 272 mg. sodium, 8 g. carb., 2 g. protein

Greek Pastries

1 (10-oz.) pkg. frozen, chopped spinach, thawed and well-drained
4 oz. feta cheese
1 medium onion, minced
2 egg whites
1/8 t. salt
1/8 t. pepper
1/8 t. nutmeg
1 (2.1)oz.) pkg Athens Foods phyllo cups (with frozen pie shells)

Mix all ingredients except phyllo cups. Fill each cup and place on baking sheet. Bake at 350 for 8 - 10 minutes. *Makes 15 at 2 fat grams and 38 calories each. 157 mg. sodium, 3 g. carb., 2 g. protein*

Baked Artichoke Dip

1 (14-oz.) can artichoke hearts, not oil-packed
1 clove garlic, minced
1/2 cup fat-free mayonnaise
dash Worcestershire
1/2 cup fat-free Parmesan cheese
black pepper to taste

Mix all ingredients in blender. Pour in pammed baking dish and bake at 350 for 20-25 minutes. Serve with fat-free crackers. (Snackwell Wheat Crackers are great.) *Serves 6 - 8 with 0 fat grams and 107 calories. 543 mg. sodium, 14 g. carb., 9 g. protein*

Chicken Fingers

These disappear fast!

2 - 3 pounds chicken tenderloins
1/4 cup skim milk
3 egg whites
1/2 cup dry bread crumbs
1/2 cup fat- free Parmesan cheese
1 t. each basil, thyme, onion powder

Mix milk and egg. In another bowl, mix bread
crumbs, Parmesan and spices. Dip chicken in milk
mix, then dredge in crumb mix. Place on heavily
pammed baking sheet and cook at 400 for 15 - 18
minutes. Serve with honey and hot mustard.

Makes about 25 at 1 fat gram and 40 calories each

Dennie's Corn Relish

2 cans black beans, drained and rinsed
1 cup frozen white corn, thawed and drained
1 cup sliced green onions
1 red pepper, chopped
1 1/2 cups picante sauce
4 oz. reduced fat Monterey Jack cheese, grated
4 T. lemon juice
1 t. cumin
1 t. olive oil

Mix all ingredients together and serve with fat-free tortilla chips. *Serves about 12 at less than 2 fat grams and 159 calories per serving. 34% C, 6 mg. sodium, 28 g. carb., 9 g. protein*

Summer Salsa

3 green onions
2 cloves garlic, or 2 t. minced garlic
1 (28-oz.) can whole tomatoes, drained and chopped or 5 fresh tomatoes, chopped
1/4 cup chopped fresh cilantro
1 t. dried oregano
1/4 t. cumin

Mix all ingredients and chill. Serve with fat-free tortilla chips. *Makes 2 cups with 0 fat grams and 32 calories. 35% C, 15 mg. sodium, 7 g. carb., 2 g.protein*

Salads

Buckhead Spinach Salad

This is a lovely and delicious presentation.

4 cups fresh spinach leaves
12 - 15 large strawberries
2 T. chopped pecans, toasted
Fat-free raspberry vinaigrette

Line four salad plates with spinach and top with strawberries. Sprinkle lightly with pecans and drizzle with dressing. Serves four at less than 1 fat gram per serving. (For company, I like to line a dinner plate with spinach leaves and put a big dollop of chicken salad in the center, surround with the berries, sprinkle all with pecans and drizzle the berries with dressing. Gorgeous!)

Serves 4 at 0 fat grams and 183 calories per serving. 57% A, 500% C, 12% calcium, 18% iron, 37 mg. sodium, 13 g. fiber, 40 g. carb., 4 g. protein.

NOTE: If the vitamins in a recipe were above 10% of the daily requirement, I included them in the nutritional data. Otherwise I just listed calories, fat, sodium, carbohydrates and proteins.

Broccoli-Red Pepper Salad

This is great with just about everything!

2 heads fresh broccoli, cut up
1 red pepper
1 yellow pepper
1/2 purple onion
Seven Seas Fat-Free Red Wine & Vinegar Salad Dressing

Steam broccoli until just barely done, then rinse in cold water.Cut up remaining vegetables then toss with about 3/4 bottle of dressing, adding more if necessary. Chill for 2 hours, toss and add more dressing if needed.
Serves 10 at 0 fat grams and 14 calories each. 12% A, 82% C, 5 mg. sodium, 3 g. carb., 1 g. protein

Broccoli Slaw

1 - 8 oz. pkg. broccoli slaw
1- 15 oz.can kidney beans, drained & rinsed
1/3 - 1/2 cup Wishbone Lite Italian dressing

Mix all ingredients together. This is great as a side dish or stuffed in a pita pocket for lunch.

Serves 6 at 0 fat grams and 115 calories per serving. 28% C, 30% calcium, 590 mg. sodium, 20 g. carb., 8 g. protein

Potato Salad

This is a tasty summer salad.

1/2 red pepper, chopped
2 pounds small red potatoes
1/3 cup green onions, chopped
1/4 cup fresh parsley, chopped
1 (10 1/2 oz) can chicken broth
1/4 cup cider vinegar
1 tablespoon dijon mustard
1 teaspoon sugar
salt & pepper to taste

Boil potatoes for 15 minutes or until tender. Drain and slice. Mix with onions and parsley.
Mix broth and remaining ingredients and bring to boil. Let cool slightly then pour over potato mixture. Cover and refrigerate overnight. Serve with slotted spoon.

Serves 12 at less than 1 fat gram and 57 calories each. 29% C, 167 mg. sodium, 12 g. carb., 2 g. protein

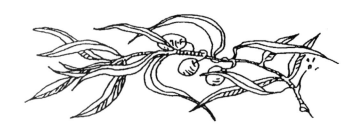

Summer Corn Salad

This is a great picnic salad!

1 (24-oz.) pkg. frozen white corn
1 cup chopped cucumber
1 cup diced tomatoes
1/4 cup chopped purple onion
1/3 cup fat-free sour cream
2 T. fat-free mayonnaise
1 T. lemon juice
1/2 t. dry mustard or Grey Poupon
salt and pepper to taste

Mix mayo, sour cream, mustard, and lemon in big bowl, then add remaining ingredients.

Serves 6 to 8 at 0 fat grams and 439 calories per serving. 126 mg. sodium, 89 g. carb., 12 g. protein

Creamy Broccoli Salad

My husband thinks this is out of this world and he doesn't really like broccoli!

1 head broccoli, chopped
1 small red onion, chopped
1 cup fat-free mayonnaise
1 T. sugar
1 T. cider vinegar
1/2 cup raisins
2 T. bacon bits
1 cup shredded fat-free cheddar cheese

Mix mayonnaise in large bowl with vinegar and sugar, then add remaining ingredients. Cover and refrigerate 3 hours.

Serves 6 at less than 1 fat gram and 124 calories per serving. 26% C, 30% calcium, 590 mg. sodium, 21 g. carb., 8 g. protein

NOTE: Broccoli stimulates the body's natural defenses to render cancer-causing chemicals harmless. Eat up!

Mandarin Black Bean Salad

This is one of my favorite salads.

1 (11-oz.)can mandarin oranges, UNdrained
2 T. red wine vinegar
1 t. dijon mustard
1/4 t. cilantro
1/8 t. cumin
1/4 t. pepper
1/2 cup diced low-fat Monterey Jack cheese
1/4 cup chopped red onion
1 t. minced garlic
1 (15-oz) can black beans, drained

Drain oranges and save 1 1/2 T. syrup. Mix syrup with vinegar, mustard, and add spices with whisk. Add remaining ingredients and toss.

Serves 4 at 2 fat grams and 359 calories each. 17% calcium, 28% iron, 58 mg. sodium, 62 g. carb., 23 g. protein

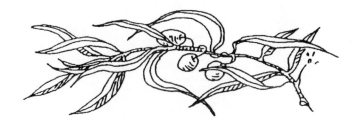

Creamy Cole Slaw

My husband loves cole slaw, and swears this one is as good as the 62 fat gram per serving variety.

1 head green cabbage, shredded
2 medium carrots, grated
1 green pepper, diced
2 T. grated onion
2 cups fat-free mayonnaise
3/4 cup sugar
1/4 cup dijon mustarad
1/4 cup cider vinegar
2 T. celery seeds
1 t. salt
1/8 t. pepper

Mix veggies, then add remaining ingredients. Toss well and chill for 3 - 4 hours before serving.
Serves 6 at 0 fat grams.

NOTE: Eat five servings of fruit and vegetables each day to prevent cancer, heart disease and lots of other diseases!

All Night Cole Slaw

My husband is a coleslaw fanatic, and he gives this two thumbs up.

6 cups shredded cabbage
3 cups shredded carrots
1 cup sliced green onions
1 cup cider vinegar
1 cup apple juice
1-1/2 tablespoons dijon mustard
1-1/2 teaspoons paprika
1 teaspoon mustard seeds
1/4 teaspoon garlic powder
salt & pepper to taste

Mix vegetables in large bowl. Combine vinegar with remaining ingredients and pour over cabbage mixture and toss well. Cover and refrigerate overnight or at least 8 hours. Serve with slotted spoon because the dressing will sit on the bottom of the bowl.

Serves 12 wtih 0 fat grams and 45 calories. 297% A, 35% C, 41 mg. sodium, 11 g. carb., 1 g. protein

Betty's Pasta Salad

I tasted this at The Catering Company and luckily got the recipe!

16-oz bottle Kraft fat-free Italian dressing
12-oz. pkg. spiral pasta
3 large tomatoes, diced
2 medium zucchini, diced
1 cucumber, diced
1 green pepper, diced
1 red pepper, diced
1 red onion, diced
2 teaspoons black pepper
1 teaspoon paprika
1/2 teaspoon celery salt
1/4 teaspoon garlic salt

Cook pasta according to directions, omitting oil if it's called for. Mix all ingredients in large bowl and toss with dressing. Betty adds black olives and sesame seeds to hers, but I omitted them here because of fat.

Serves 6 - 8 at less than 1 fat gram and 240 calories per serving. 48% C, 147 mg. sodium, 58 g. carb., 4 g. protein

More Ellen Moore Pasta Salad

This makes for a delicious, nutritious lunch!

12 oz. bag spiral tri-color pasta
1 large Vidalia onion, chopped
1 yellow pepper, chopped
1 carrot, shredded
2 stalks celery, chopped
1 can kidney beans, rinsed & drained
1/2 cup fat-free Parmesan cheese
1 (1.05 oz) packet Fat Free Good Seasons Dressing, mixed to directions
1/2 cup fat-free Ranch dressing

Cook and drain pasta. Mix with vegetables, then toss with Good Seasons and Ranch dressings. Refrigerate.

Serves 8 at less than 1 fat gram and 213 calories per serving. 50% A, 17% iron, 210 mg. sodium, 41 g. carb., 10 g. protein

Tisho's Roasted Pepper Pasta Salad

This is easier to make than it sounds and can be a main dish with the addition of 2 cups of grilled chicken or shrimp.

12-oz bag spiral tri-color pasta
1 red pepper, halved
1 yellow pepper, halved
1 large vidalia onion, sliced
1 pound frozen baby peas
1 can artichokes, packed in water
16-oz bottle Wishbone Lite Italian
1/2 cup Parmesan cheese

Spray baking sheet with cooking spray and place peppers and onions on it. Bake at 375 until peppers are blackened and onions are roasted. Peel black off peppers and slice. Cook and drain pasta and rinse with water. Toss pasta with peppers, onions, peas, sliced artichokes and add dressing and Parmesan. Chill and serve with homegrown tomatoes. Serves 12 at less than 1 fat gram per serving.

Black Bean & Chicken Salad

This has a Southwestern taste, and is delicious!

1 green pepper, chopped
1 red pepper, chopped
2 cloves garlic, minced
1 red onion, chopped
1 teaspoon oregano
1/2 teaspoon cumin
1/4 cup sherry
1 teaspoon chicken bouillon granules
2 large tomatoes, chopped
2 cups chicken, chopped
2 -15 oz. cans black beans, drained
1 cup frozen corn
salt and pepper to taste
dash Tabasco

Spray non-stick skillet with cooking spray and saute peppers, onions and garlic. Add sherry, bouillon and spices. Add beans, tomatoes, chicken and corn to mixture. Season. Cover and refrigerate.

Serves 6 at 2 fat grams and 326 calories per serving. 21% A, 70% C, 23% iron, 247 mg. sodium, 11 g. fiber, 46 g. carb., 29 g. protein

Summer Chicken Salad

This is a winner!

3 boneless, skinless chicken breasts
1 bay leaf
1 carrot
1 small onion, peeled
1 t. garlic or 1 clove, peeled
1/4 cup fat-free mayonnaise
1/4 cup plain fat-free yogurt
1 T. lemon juice
2 t. sugar
1 cup chopped celery
1 cup seedless red grapes, halved
1 yellow pepper,finely chopped
1/4 cup green onion, chopped

Boil chicken with bay leaf, carrot, onion and 1 t. garlic.
Cut up chicken when done. Mix yogurt, mayo, lemon
& sugar, and toss with chicken and veggies.

Serves 6 at 2 fat grams and 167 calories per serving.
84% C, 98 mg. sodium, 9 g. carb., 27 g. protein

Chicken Waldorf Salad

This is a beautiful presentation and is delicious as well.

4 boneless, skinless chicken breasts
1 celery stalk
1 garlic clove
1 carrot
peeled onion
2 large red delicious apples
1 T. lemon juice
4 large stalks celery, chopped
1/2 cup raisins
1/3 cup fat-free mayonnaise
1/3 cup plain fat-free yogurt
2 t. sugar
1 T.   chopped pecans, toasted
Cavender's Greek Seasoning to taste (with spices at grocery store)

Simmer chicken with celery stalk, garlic clove, carrot and peeled onion until chicken is done. Remove chicken and cut up. Chop apples, leaving peel on and sprinkle with lemon juice. Mix mayonnaise, yogurt and sugar, then combine all ingredients and mix well. Season to taste with Cavender's. Spread pecans on baking sheet and run under broiler for a minute until toasted. (This brings out flavor so we can get by with less!) Sprinkle each serving lightly with pecans. Garnish plates with red grapes and leaf lettuce if desired.

Serves 8 at 3 fat grams and 112 calories each. 50 mg. sodium, 14 g. carb., 11 g. protein

Tropical Chicken Salad

This is very low in fat and yummy as well!

2 boneless, skinless chicken breasts, cooked & cut up
2 T fat-free red wine oil & vinegar salad dressing
1 1/2 cups cooked brown rice
3 stalks celery, chopped
1/4 red pepper, chopped
1/4 cup green onion, chopped
1/4 cup fat-free mayonnaise
1/4 cup fat-free plain yogurt
1/2 cantaloupe, chopped
Cavender's Greek Seasoning (with spices at grocery)

Pour salad dressing over chicken. Mix mayo with yo-gurt and mix with chicken. Add remaining ingredients. Season to taste with Cavender's .

Serves 4 with 2 fat grams and 479 calories per serving. 30% A, 45% C, 700mg. sodium, 81 g. carb., 28 g. pro-tein

Carrot Raisin Salad

1 - 8 oz. can crushed pineapple, UNdrained
1-8 oz. pkg. grated carrots
1/2 cup raisins
3/4 cup vanilla nonfat yogurt
1 teaspoon sugar

Mix all and refrigerate.

*Serves 6 at 0 fat grams and 80 calories each. 190%
A, 11% C, 27 mg. sodium, 17 g. carb., 2 g. protein*

Black Bean Salsa

*This disappears as fast as I make it, and that's
okay because it's so easy!*

1-15 oz.can black beans, drained & rinsed
1- 10 oz. pkg. frozen white corn
1 -15 oz. can Mexican tomatoes, NOT drained
1 tablespoon fresh cilantro

Mix all together and refrigerate. This is great on low-
fat tortilla chips and as a side dish for grilled meats.

*Serves 6 at 0 fat grams and 125 calories each. 5 mg.
sodium, 24 mg. carb., 8 g. protein*

Sally's Tuna Salad

I tasted this at my sister-in-law's, and had to have the recipe.

1 -12 oz can albacore tuna
1-8 oz. carton fat-free cottage cheese
1 tablespoon lemon juice
1 small red onion, chopped
2 hardboiled eggs, yolk removed
1 tablespoon dried dill
salt & pepper to taste
Cavender's Greek Seasoning to taste

Drain and rinse tuna. Discard yolk from eggs and chop whites. Mix all ingredients in large bowl and refrigerate.

Serves 6 at 2 fat grams and 98 calories each. 437 mg. sodium, 2 g. carb., 20 g. protein.

NOTE: Try to eat more fish! Just 2 ounces of fish a week reduces the risk of heart disease substantially. I hate to cook it so I order it when I eat out.

Soups

Herb-Barley Soup

This is a comforting, tasty soup.

2 onions, chopped
6 bouillon cubes
2 quarts of water
1/2 cup barley
1 T. basil
1 bay leaf
1 t. paprika
1 pound fresh mushrooms, sliced
1 (16-oz.) can tomatoes

Place bouillon cubes in soup pot and add 1/4 cup water. Add onions and saute until done. Add rest of water, barley and seasonings. Simmer for 1 hour, stirring some. Add tomatoes and mushrooms and simmer 20 minutes.

Serves 8 at 1 fat gram each. 1340 mg. sodium, 18 g. carb, 5 g. protein

French Onion Soup

I served this on Christmas Eve and my brother, who is spoiled by the restaurants in NYC, went back for thirds.

2 cans beef broth
1 clove garlic, crushed
3 large yellow onions
4 thick slices French bread
1/2 cup reduced fat Swiss cheese
1/4 cup Parmesan cheese

Saute onion and garlic in pammed Dutch oven, covered. Add broth and simmer 30 minutes. Top bread slices with Swiss cheese, then sprinkle with Parmesan and run under broiler. When toasted, put a slice on each bowl of soup.

Serves 4 at 4 fat grams and 162 calories each. 21% calcium, 1556 mg. sodium, 19 g. carb., 14 g. protein.

NOTE: If your soup is too salty, try throwing in a whole peeled potato for 10 minutes, then remove it before serving.

NOTE: *To reduce sodium, use sodium-free or low-sodium beef broth or bouillon cubes.*

Cuban Black Bean Soup

This is just delicious.

1 lb. dried black beans
9 cups water
2 t. minced garlic
1/4 t. salt
1 green pepper, chopped
2 onions, chopped
2 T. lemon juice
1 1/2 t. cumin
1/2 t. oregano
2-4 drops hot sauce (optional)

Sort and wash beans. Place in large dutch oven and cover with water. Soak overnight, then drain and return to pan. Add 9 cups water, 2 t. garlic and salt. Bring to boil, then cover and reduce heat and simmer 2 hours until tender. Add remaining ingredients and simmer 35 - 45 more minutes, stirring occasionally. Serve over cooked rice and garnish with chopped onion.

Serves 8 at 1 fat gram and 204 calories per serving.17% C, 215 mg. sodium, 38 g. carb., 13 g. protein.

Clara's Cabbage Soup

This was my neighbor Clara Bole's recipe, and I loved both it and her. My husband begs me to make this soup.

2 onions, chopped
1 green pepper, chopped
1 46-oz. can V-8 juice
3 stalks celery, chopped
2 T. minced parsley
1 T. Worcestershire sauce
1 whole lemon with peel on
salt & pepper to taste
1 T. garlic, minced
3 beef bouillon cubes
2 cans red beans
2 cans stewed tomatoes
1 head cabbage, chopped
2 cups water

Saute onions, pepper, celery and garlic in 1/4 cup V-8 juice. Add remaining ingredients, except beans. Simmer 45 minutes. Add beans, cook until beans are warm.   *Serves 10 - 12 at less than 1 fat gram and 190 calories each. 39% A, 148% C, 14% calclium, 25% iron, 1007 mg. sodium, 10 g. fiber, 37 g. carb.,, 12 g. protein*
(Clara used to make this with hamburger meat. If you can spare the fat, start with a pound of very lean chopped sirloin in the pot. When cooked, drain the meat and add the veggies and follow the rest of the recipe the same. Be sure and account for the extra fat!)

Mother's Bean Soup

This is my mother's prized recipe and you wouldn't believe how hard it was for me to get!

1 pkg. (20 oz.) 15 bean mix
2 quarts water
2 onions, chopped
2 t. minced garlic
2 stalks celery, chopped
4 chicken bouillon cubes
1(15-oz.) can tomatoes
1/8 t. cayenne
1 T. each basil and parsley
juice of 1 lemon
salt and pepper to taste

Cover beans with water and soak overnight. Drain and rinse in collander. In soup pot, saute onions, garlic and celery with Pam. When tender add beans and 2 quarts of water. Add bouillon cubes and simmer for 2 1/2 to 3 hours. Add tomatoes and seasonings. Simmer 30 more minutes. Add juice of 1 lemon right before serving.

Serves 10 - 12 at 2 fat grams and 209 calories per serving. 17% C, 22 % iron, 654 mg. sodium, 38 g. carb., 14 g. protein

(Mother says the lemon is the kicker here, but if you add it too early it will make the soup bitter; however, it reheats just fine.)

Eileen's Minnesota Minestrone

The first time I made this soup was during the ice storm that immobilized Chattanooga in 1996 .Frustrated pioneers, we stuck it out with no electricity or heat, while the temperature dropped below freezing. This warmed us up in spirit and body.

4 cups water
2 cups chopped carrots
1-15 oz. can white beans, rinsed and drained
1 can garbonzo beans, rinsed and drained
1-14 oz can tomatoes, cut up
1 cup chopped onion
3 chicken bouillon cubes
1 teaspoon minced garlic
1/2 teaspoon dried basil
1/2 teaspoon dried oregano
salt & pepper to taste
9-oz pkg. frozen green beans or 14.5 oz can
1 medium zucchini, chopped
1/2 cup broken spaghetti, NOT cooked
 6 tablespoons parmesan cheese

Put water, carrots, beans, tomatoes, onion, boullion, garlic and seasonings in large pot. Bring to boil, then add green beans, zucchini and pasta and bring to boil again. Reduce heat, cover and simmer for 10 minutes or until pasta is done. Sprinkle each serving with Parmesan cheese. Serves 6 at 2 fat grams and 322 calories each. 400% A, 35% C, 710 mg. sodium 60 g. carb., 18 g. protein

Katie's Black Bean Soup

This is super-quick and easy!

1- 12-oz. can Black Bean Soup (Progresso)
1 15 oz. can black beans (drained)
1 1/2 cups water
1 cup medium salsa
1 tsp. sherry vinegar (or to taste)

Combine soup, beans, water and salsa. Bring to a simmer and cook, uncovered, 20 - 30 minutes. Stir in vinegar right before serving. Top with fat-free sour cream and sliced green onions.

Serves 6 at 2 fat grams per serving and 196 calories • 17% iron • 300 mg. sodium • 35 g. carb. • 12 g. protein

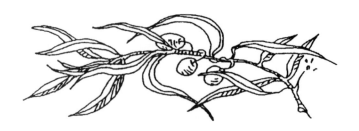

Ice Storm Chili

Another keeper from the ice storm. Luckily this one's super-quick and easy because my hands were so cold I could barely keep them out of my pockets long enough to make this.

28-oz can tomatoes, cut up
3 (15 1/2 oz) cans chili beans rinsed and drained
12-oz can light beer or nonalcoholic beer
1 onion, chopped

Put all ingredients in saucepan and bring to boil. Reduce heat and simmer, uncovered for 15 minutes. Serve topped with fat-free sour cream (Guilt Free), a little chopped green onion and fat-free cheddar cheese.

Serves 4 with 1 fat gram and 500 calories per serving. 31% C, 22% calcium, 65% iron, 178 mg. sodium • 88 g. carb., 33 g. protein

Spicy White Chili

1 pound white beans, washed & sorted
2 boneless, skinless chicken breasts
7 cups water
2 cloves garlic
4 chicken bouillon cubes
2 onions, chopped
2 t. cumin
1/4 t. ground cloves
1/4 t. cayenne pepper
salt to taste

Put beans, water and chicken in large pot with boullion cubes and bring to boil. Reduce heat and simmer until chicken is done. Take out chicken and cut up, then put back in pot and add remaining ingredients. Simmer 3 hours, until beans are tender. Add more water if necessary.
To serve, top with chopped green onions and fat-free shredded cheddar cheese.

Serves 6 at 2 fat grams and 296 calories each.
21% calcium • 46% iron • 12 g. fiber •
478 g. carb. • 25 g. protein

Cowboy Corn Chowder

This is hearty, spicy and delicious!

1 large yellow onion
1 Louis Rich kielbasa sausage, sliced
2 large potatoes, peeled and chopped
2 cups water
1 stalk celery, diced
1/2 green pepper, diced
1/2 cup green onion, chopped
1 (14.5 oz.) can creamed corn
2 T. minced garlic
2 T. parsley
2 T. oregano
2 bay leaves
2 cups water
2 cups fat-free buttermilk

Spray non-stick skillet with cooking spray and saute onion with 1/8 cup water. When translucent, add sausage and brown. When done, add potatoes and 2 cups water. Cover and cook 15 minutes or so until potatoes are tender. Then add celery, pepper, green onion, corn, garlic, parsley, oregano, bay leaves two more cups water and simmer for 15 minutes on low until heated through. If you are not ready to serve it, let it stay on low heat, then when time to eat, add buttermilk and heat on low heat until soup is warmed. Add salt and pepper and red pepper to taste and enjoy!

Serves 4 - 6 at 2 fat grams and 180 calories each. 34% C, 13% calcium, 601 mg. sodium, 15 g. carb., 8 g. protein

Tarragon Chicken Soup

This soup is the essence of comfort.

2 boneless, skinless chicken breasts
2 stalks celery
outer peel of onion
1 carrot
1 t. garlic, minced
7 cups water
4 chicken bouillon cubes
4 oz. egg noodles
1 large onion, chopped
2 stalks celery, chopped
2 carrots, sliced
1/2 t. salt
1/2 t. pepper
1/2 t. tarragon

Cook chicken in water with next 6 ingredients. Let simmer 45 minutes. Remove chicken, celery, onion and carrot and cut up chicken. Put back in pot and add veggies and seasoning and simmer 15 minutes. Add noodles and simmer 10 minutes or until done.

Serves 10 at 2 grams of fat and 76 calories per serving. 73% A, 546 mg. sodium, 11 g. carb., 6 g. protein

Marty's Spinach Soup

When I first moved to Lookout Mountain as a newly-wed, I was apprehensive about my new neighborhood. My sister-in-law brought over a big pot of this soup, and it was almost as comforting as she was!

2-(13 1/2-oz.) cans chicken broth
1-10-oz pkg. frozen chopped spinach
1 onion, chopped
1 8-oz. pkg. fat-free cream cheese, softened

Bring chicken broth to boil, then add spinach and onion to broth. When onion is cooked, add cream cheese. Puree in small batches in blender or food processor. Return to pot and heat. Serve with fat-free croutons.

Serves 6 at 0 fat grams and 89 calories per serving. 85% A, 21% C, 18% calcium, 969 mg. sodium, 6 g. carb., 12 g. protein

Turkey and Wild Rice Soup

1- 5 oz. pkg. wild rice mix
2 cans chicken broth
1 cup turkey breast, chopped
1 onion minced
1 cup mushrooms, chopped

Saute mushrooms and onion in 1/4 cup broth, covered in kettle. Add rest of ingredients. Serves 4 - 6 at less than 1 fat gram and 154 calories. 935 mg sodium.

Totally Tortilla Soup

A very satisfying Mexican soup.

2 cans reduced fat chicken broth
1/2 cup chopped celery
1 can Mexican tomatoes (or stewed
 tomatoes with 1 t. chili powder)
1/2 cup chopped onion
3 cloves garlic, minced
2 t. chopped fresh cilantro (or parsley if you
 don't like cilantro)
shredded fat-free Mexican cheese
fat-free or low fat tortilla chips

In pot, bring broth, celery, onions and garlic to boil.
Add rest of ingredients, except cheese and tortillas.
Put a few chips in bowls, serve soup, then top with
cheese. Serves 4.

Tina's Gazpacho

My good friend adapted this wonderful recipe for The Gorgeless Gourmet Newsletter. It is healthy as well as yummy!

8 tomatoes
4 cucumbers, peeled
4 Vidalia onions, peeled
4 green peppers, seeded
8 oz. cider vinegar
2 pkg. Good Seasons fat-free Italian dressing mix
1-46 oz. can V-8 juice

In food processor chop vegetables with pulse button - do not puree. Mix dressing mix with 1/4 cup water and add to vinegar. Combine all in large bowl and add V-8 juice. Cover and let sit overnight.

Serves 12-14 at 0 fat grams and 109 calories per serving. 41% C, 116% A, 904 mg. sodium, 18 g. carb., 3 g. protein

This also makes an awesome salsa to dip with lowfat tortilla chips —just delete the V-8 and add fresh cilantro.

White Bean and Sausage Soup

This is hearty and delicious.

olive oil cooking spray (or any fat-free cooking spray)
1 large onion
1 T. garlic, minced
2 stalks celery, chopped
1 Louis Rich kielbasa sausage, (7 oz) sliced
1 (8-oz.) can tomato sauce
1 (15-oz.) can white beans
2 chicken bouillon cubes
2 cups water
2 bay leaves

Spray stock pot with cookng spray and saute onion, celery and garlic. When done add sausage and to-mato sauce. Simmer about 20 minutes. Add beans, water, bouillon cubes and bay leaves. Simmer about 1 hour.

Serves 6 at less than 1 fat gram and 318 calories per serving. 19% C, 20% calcium, 45% iron, 929 mg. sodium, 48 g. carb., 20 g. protein

NOTE: If you want a thicker soup, mash up some of the beans before serving.

Vegetables

Bab's Squash Casserole

This was one of the first recipes a reader submitted.

2 cups cooked yellow squash
1/2 cup liquid butter buds
3 egg whites
1 t. salt
1/4 t. pepper
1/2 cup chopped onion
1 cup shredded fat-free cheddar cheese
1 cup evaporated SKIM milk
1 cup crushed fat-free saltines

Mash squash and add remaining ingredients. Mix well. Pour into Pammed 1 quart casserole and bake at 375 for about 40 minutes.

Serves 6 at less than 1 fat gram and 87 calories per serving. 37% C, 38% calcium, 617 mg. sodium, 10 g. carb., 11 g. protein

Creamy Cheesy Squash

This tastes very, very rich!

2 pounds yellow squash, about 5 medium
1 large onion, chopped
1 t. sugar
1/4 lb. Light Velveeta Cheese
1 small green pepper, chopped

Boil squash and onion until tender, then add pepper
and boil one minute. Drain well and add sugar, salt,
pepper and cheese. Pour into pammed casserole and
bake at 350 for 15 minutes. Stir and serve.

*Serves 4 at 3 fat grams and 135 calories per serving.
78% C, 26% calcium, 316 mg. sodium, 13 g. carb., 10
g. protein*

NOTE: This does not set up, but is loose like pudding.

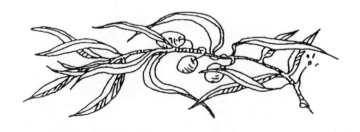

Cheesy Spinach-Artichoke Casserole

This is a given at our holiday table!

1 can artichokes, packed in water, quartered
2 pkg. chopped spinach, thawed & drained
1 onion, minced
1 8-oz. block fat-free cream cheese
1/4 cup skim milk
1/2 cup fat-free Parmesan cheese

Mix spinach with cream cheese, Parmesan cheese, onion and skim milk. Pour into Pammed casserole, then top with artichokes. Sprinkle with more Parmesan and bake at 350 degrees for 40 minutes, covered. Uncover and bake 10 minutes.

Serves 6 at 0 fat grams and 72 calories per serving. 104% A, 36% C, 22% calcium, 376 mg. sodium, 8 g. carb., 9 g. protein

Andrea's Cheesy Broccoli

This is so easy and really good! It's a great way to get brown rice and broccoli in my kids.

1 (16-oz.) pkg Green Giant Broccoli & Cheese
1/2 cup fat-free cottage cheese
1 bag 10-minute Boil -In-Bag brown rice
1/2 cup fat-free cheddar cheese

Do not cook rice. Mix broccoli, cottage cheese and rice and pour into pammed casserole. Bake at 350 for 45 minutes or until bubbly. Top with cheddar and let sit on top of stove until cheese melts.

Serves 6 at 2 fat grams and 248 calories per serving. 27% A, 117% C, 38% calcium, 270 mg. sodium, 34 g. carb., 15 g. protein.

Cheesy Tomato Pie

This is rich and tasty!

2 cups shredded potatoes, thawed (Ore Ida)
2 egg whites
1 tablespoon Parmesan

3 - 4 fresh tomatoes, sliced
3/4 cup fat-free Parmesan
3/4 cup fat-free mozzarella
1 tablespoon dried basil or to taste
salt & pepper to taste

Mix potatoes, egg whites and 1 T. Parmesan and spread in pammed pie pan. Bake at 350 for 15 - 20 minutes. Put half of each cheese on bottom of pie shell. Layer tomato slices on top and sprinkle with salt, pepper, basil and remaining Parmesan. Bake at 350 for 30 minutes. Top with rest of mozzarella and let sit until melted.

Serves 6 at 0 fat grams and 121 calories. 12% A, 30% C, 34% calcium, 365 mg. sodium, 14 g. carb., 13 g. protein

NOTE: Tomatoes are loaded with vitamins C and A and are at the top of the list of cancer preventers.

Migrit's Corn Pudding

This is Margaret Kelley's recipe and it is almost as well loved as she is!

1 can creamed corn
1 can whole kernel corn, drained
1 (8 oz.) tub sour cream
3 egg whites
1 box Jiffy corn muffin mix
1 cup fat-free or reduced fat cheddar cheese

Mix all together except cheese and pour into pammed casserole. Bake at 375 for 20 minutes. Top with cheese.
Serves 8 at 4 fat grams and 132 calories per serving. 25% calcium, 371 mg. sodium, 20 g. carb., 8 g. protein

Jan's Corn Pudding

My sister-in-law, who has catered for former President Carter, made this one up.

2 cups fat-free vanilla yogurt
16 oz. bag frozen white corn
5 egg whites
salt and pepper to taste

Mix egg whites, seasonings and yogurt, then add corn. Pour into pammed casserole and bake at 350 for 45 minutes.
Serves 6 at 0 fat grams and 72 calories each. 443 mg. sodium, 10 g. carb., 7 g. protein.

Nat's Green Beans

These taste like you spent hours stringing and used tons of fat cooking them.

1 20-oz. can Allans' Green Beans
1 tablespoon Hormel Bacon Bits
1/4 cup brown sugar
1/4 cup red wine vinegar
1 large onion, sliced and rings separated
garlic salt to taste

Drain and rinse beans and put in sauce pan. Add rest of ingredients, cover and simmer one hour or all afternoon, the longer the better. Add a little water if necessary.

Serves 6 at 0 fat grams and 49 calories per serving. 493 mg. sodium, 11 g. carb., 2 g. protein

Very Vidalia Casserole

This is a great way to take advantage of those yummy Vidalia onions. It's very rich tasting and my husband went wild over it.

5 large Vidalia onions, sliced
1/2 cup fat-freeParmesan cheese
1/2 cup reduced-fat Ritz cracker crumbs
1/2 cup reduced fat "Cheese-It" cracker crumbs
1 can reduced-fat cream of mushroom soup
1 cup fat- free grated cheddar cheese

In large skillet, "saute" onions in 1/4 cup water, covered, until limp. In pammed 2-quart casserole, layer half of onions, 1/4 cup Parmesan, 1/2 of both cracker crumbs. Season with salt and pepper and repeat layers. Spread soup over all and bake at 350 for 40 minutes until hot and bubbly. Serves 6 at 3 fat grams and 119 calories. 41% calcium, 956 mag. sodium, 12 g. carb., 11 g. protein

NOTE: Campbell's Healthy Request is the lowest fat cream of mushroom soup I know of.

Spicy Zucchini

Even my picky boys eat this!

1 t. minced garlic
1 red onion, chopped
4 - 6 medium zucchini, chopped
1 chicken bouillon cube
1/8 cup water
1/2 t. dried basil
1/2 t. dried oregano
1/2 t. dried rosemary
salt and pepper to taste

Crumble bouillon cube in nonstick skillet with water. Add garlic and onion. When onion is done, add squash and sprinkle with herbs. Cover and stir every now and then. Cook until the squash is tender, about five minutes.

Serves 4 at 0 fat grams and 42 calories per serving. 32% C, 295 mg. sodium, 9 g. carb., 3 g. protein

NOTE: We love to have this with Three Cheese Stuffed Potatoes.

Sally's Zucchini

My sister-in-law raves about this one!

1-16 oz. can creamed corn
3 cups grated zucchini
1 cup fat-free saltines, crushed
1 cup fat-free cheddar cheese
1 onion, chopped
3 egg whites
salt & pepper to taste

Mix all ingredients and pour in pammed 8x10 casserole. Bake at 350 for 1 hour.

Serves 6 at 0 fat grams and 116 calories per serving. 23% C, 15% calcium, 544 mg. sodium, 11 6. carb., 15 g. protein

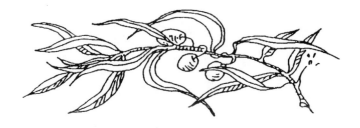

Zucchini Boats

These are hearty enough for a main dish; just add corn pudding and you're set!

4 medium zucchini
1/2 cup chopped mushrooms
1 onion, chopped
1 t. minced garlic
1/2 chopped tomato
2 egg whites
1/4 t. marjoram
1 t. parsley
1/2 cup fat-free cheddar cheese

Wash zucchini and boil for 10 m inutes, then split length-wise. Remove pulp and chop. Saute garlic, onion and mushrooms in non-stick skillet, covered, with 1/8 cup water. Add herbs, tomato and zucchini pulp. Cool and mix in egg whites, then stuff each half and bake at 350 for 30 minutes. Top with cheese.

Serves 4 at 0 fat grams and 59 calories each. 14% A, 28% C, 24% calcium, 282 mg. sodium, 7 g. carb., 8 g. protein

Spring Veggies

These are delicious any time of year!

1 bunch asparagus (14-16 stalks)
2 yellow squash
1/2 cup shredded carrots
1 t. minced garlic
1 chicken bouillon cube
1/4 cup water
1/8 t. thyme
1/2 t. oregano

Dissolve bouillon in water, and "saute" veggies with spice, covering to keep moisture in. When tender, sprinkle with Parmesan and salt to taste.

Serves 4 at 0 fat grams and 59 calories each. 167% A, 51% C, 301 mg. sodium, 12 g. carb., 5 g. protein

NOTE: If you're serious about your health, especially concerning heart disease, I highly recommend Dr. Dean Ornish's book ***How to Reverse Heart Disease.*** It's informative and very encouraging.

Roasted Tomato Mashed Potatoes

I had these at the Union Square Cafe in New York and tried my best to copy them. This is pretty close.

3 potatoes, scrubbed and cut up
2 tomatoes, halved
1 T. minced garlic
1/2 cup fat-free sour cream
1 cup low-fat cottage cheese
1/4 cup fat-free Parmesan cheese
2 T. fat-free butter

Spray pan with Pam and brush tomatoes with garlic. Bake at 350 for 20-30 minutes, then put in bowl. Boil and drain potatoes and mash with tomatoes. Add remaining ingredients.

Serves 6 at 0 fat grams and 108 calories per serving. 26% C, 255 mg. sodium, 16 g. carb., 9 g. protein

Garlic Mashed Potatoes

My husband could eat these every night.

3 large baking potatoes
3 cloves garlic, peeled
2 chicken bouillon cubes
1 cup fat-free cottage cheese
1/2 cup fat-free Parmesan cheese
1 tablespoon fat-free butter
salt & pepper to taste

Peel potatoes and put in large pot. Cover with water and add bouillon cubes and garlic cloves. Bring to boil and cook until potatoes are done. Drain well then pour in bowl. While hot, add cottage cheese, Parmesan, fat-free butter, salt and pepper and beat with mixer.

Serves 6-8 at 0 fat grams and 106 calories per serving. 15% C, 680 mg. sodium, 13 g. carb., 10 g. protein

NOTE: Garlic is touted as a natural antibiotic and works to lower LDL (bad cholesterol) while raising HDL (good cholesterol).

Buttermilk Mashed Potatoes

Yet another recipe for mashed potatoes!

2 large potatoes
2 whole cloves garlic
3 chicken bouillon cubes
1 cup fat-free buttermilk
1 T. fat-free margarine
salt & pepper to taste

Wash, peel and chop potatoes. Put in saucepan and cover with water. Add peeled garlic cloves and bouillon cubes and bring to boil .Simmer until potatoes are done, about 30 minutes. Drain and mix remaining ingredients into potatoes with mixer.

Serves 4 with 0 fat grams and 68 calories per serving. 16% C, 953 mg. sodium, 12 g. carb., 4 g. protein

Potatoes No Gratin

These are as rich and creamy as the fat-loaded kind!

2 large potatoes, peeled and thinly sliced
1 large onion, thinly sliced
1/4 cup fat-free Parmesan cheese
2 tablespoons fat-free butter
3 slices fat-free American cheese
salt and pepper to taste
1/2 cup skim milk

In 2 qt. casserole, layer 1/2 potatoes, 1/2 onion, and
ALL American cheese. Repeat layers, then sprinkle top
with butter , Parmesan and seasonings. Pour milk over
top, then cover tightly with lid or foil and bake at 350 for
1 hour or until done.

*Serves 6 at 0 fat grams and 74 calories per serving.
28% calcium, 285 mg. sodium, 10 g. carb., 8 g. protein*

Hash Brown Potatoes

This tastes just as fried as it can be!

Fat-Free cooking spray
2/3 pkg.(2 lb) frozen shredded potatoes (Ore Ida)
1 onion, minced
1 clove garlic, minced
1/4 t. dried thyme
1/8 t. pepper

Thaw and drain potatoes, then mix all ingredients. Spray 10 " non-stick skillet with cooking spray and heat pan over medium heat. Pack potato mixture into pan and cook for 6 - 7 minutes or until brown on bottom. Carefully invert plate onto patty and pick up skillet and turn potato patty onto plate. Carefully slip the patty, uncooked side down, back into skillet and cook 6 - 7 more minutes. Cut into 4 wedges and serve with ketchup.

Serves 4 at 0 fat grams and 108 calories per serving. 45% C, 145 mg. sodium, 25 g. carb., 3 g. protein

Ratatouille Topped Potatoes

This is yummy, nutritious and so easy!

1 egg plant, washed and cut up
3 each, yellow squash & zucchnni, sliced
1 can stewed tomatoes
1 large onion, chopped
2 t. minced garlic
1 bay leaf
1/2 t. EACH thyme & rosemary
6 baking potatoes

Put all vegetables except potatoes in pammed casserole. Cover and bake at 400 for 1 1/2 hours. Bake potatoes at same time; just prick with a fork and bake for the last hour. Top each potato with Ratatouille and Parmesan!

Serves 6 at 0 fat grams and 133 calories. 65% C, 209 mg. sodium, 30 g. carb., 4 g. protein

Three Cheese Stuffed Potatoes

We have these about once a week!

4 large baking potatoes
1 pound fat-free cottage cheese
1 T. grated onion
1/2 cup fat-free Parmesean cheese
1/2 cup fat-free Cheddar cheese
salt and pepper to taste

Bake potatoes, then scoop out insides and immediately mix with cottage cheese. Add remaining ingredients, mix, and fill potato shells. Bake at 350 for 20 minutes. Top with more Parmesan cheese.

Serves 4 at 0 fat grams and 251 calories per serving. 37% C, 40% calcium, 789 mg. sodium, 30 g. carb., 26 g. protein

Loaded Baked Potatoes

These taste like the packed-with-fat variety!

4 large baking potatoes, washed
3/4 cup low-fat cottage cheese
3 ounces Light Velveeta Cheese
3 T. Bac-os (Betty Crocker bacon bits)
salt and pepper to taste

Prick potatoes with fork and bake at 400 for about one hour until done. Slice of tops and scoop out hot potato. Mix with cottage cheese, Velveeta, Bac-os and seasonings, then stuff back into potato and heat at 350 for about 15 minutes.

Serves 4 at 3 fat grams and 163 calories each. 28% C, 15% calcium, 474 mg. sodium, 18 g. carb., 14 g. protein

Sweet Potato Boats

These are staples at our Thanksgiving dinners.

6 small sweet potatoes
4 egg whites
3/4 cup brown sugar, divided
3 T. fat-free butter
1/2 cup crushed corn flakes mixed with 1/4 cup brown sugar
1 16-oz. can crushed pineapple, undrained

Prick potatoes with fork and bake until tender at 375 (1 hour). Slice tops off and scrape out potato, leaving shells intact. Mash potatoes with 1/2 cup sugar, egg whites, pineapple and fat-free butter, then stuff back into shells. Top with cornflake crumb mixture, then bake at 350 for 35 minutes. For canned potatoes, pour into pammed 9x13 pan and top with topping.

Serves 6 at 0 fat grams and 207 calories per serving. 281% A, 46% C, 121 mg. sodium, 48 g. carb., 4 g. protein

Tuscany White Beans

You can use two cans of beans to save time; just rinse them to reduce sodium.

1 pound dried white beans
8 cups water
2 bay leaves
2 cloves garlic
1 t. dried thyme
3 tomatoes or 1 can diced tomatoes
2 cups chicken broth
2 T. dried parsley

Rinse and sort beans and soak in water overnight. Rinse again and place in large stock pot with 8 cups water, garlic and bay leaves. Bring to boil, then reduce heat and simmer until beans are tender, about 45 minutes. Skim off any foam that rises to top. Drain beans and discard bay leaves. Pour back in pot and add thyme, tomatoes and broth. Cook on medium for 10 minutes. Season with salt and pepper and serve with crusty French bread.

Serves 6 at 0 fat grams and 291 calories each. 18% A, 20% calcium, 47% iron, 548 mg. sodium, 50 g. carb., 22 g. protein

Curt's Hoppin' John

Eating blackeyed peas on New Years' Day brings good luck for the new year.

1 cup black-eyed peas
6 cups water
3 slices turkey bacon
1 cup chopped onion
1 clove garlic, minced
1 cup white rice, not instant
2 t. salt
1 t. pepper
1/4 t. red pepper

Rinse black-eyed peas and put in water. Boil 2 minutes, then let stand 1 hour. In Dutch oven, cook bacon, onion and garlic, but do not let veggies get too brown. Take out bacon when crisp and crumble. Add peas, rice, seasoning and liquid to cooking pot and bring to boil. Then reduce heat, cover and simmer 1 hour. When beans are tender and rice is done, put in bacon and serve. Serves 4-6 at 1 fat gram per serving.

Susan's Black Baked Beans

This has a smokey, porky taste due to the sun-dried tomatoes.

2 cans black beans, drained
1 (14.5 oz.) can stewed tomatoes
1 large onion, chopped
6-8 sun-dried tomatoes, (not in oil, chopped)
1/4 cup molasses
salt and pepper to taste

Mix all ingredients together in a baking dish. Stir well.Cover and bake at 350 for one hour.

Serves 6 at less than 1 fat gram and 460 calories per serving. 20% A, 68% calcium, 60%, 1702 mg. sodium, 93 g. carb., 25 g. protein

NOTE: To reduce sodium in canned goods, rinse vegetables under running water for one minute. It reduces it by about half.

Bacon Baked Beans

These are really yummy and I never have leftovers!

1 onion chopped
1/2 cup brown sugar
1/2 cup tomato sauce
1 T. molasses
1 T. cider vinegar
1 T. Worcestershire sauce
1 (15-oz.) can light red kidney beans, drained
1 (15-oz) can dark red kidney beans, drained
1 (15-oz) can white beans, drained
salt & pepper to taste
3 strips turkey bacon

Mix all ingredients except bacon and pour into a pammed baking dish. Lay bacon over beans and bake at 350 for 1 hour.

Serves 8 at 1 fat gram and 533 calories each. 25% calcium, 70% iron, 337 mg. sodium, 92 g. carb., 36 g. protein

The Best Baked Beans

These are out-of-this world and I'm not kidding!

1/2 pound light or turkey sausage
1 onion, chopped
1/2 cup brown sugar
1/2 cup tomato sauce
1 T. molasses
1 T. cider vinegar
1 T. Worcestershire sauce
1 (15-oz.) can butter beans, well drained
1 (15-oz.) can light red kidney beans, well drained
1 (15-0z.) can dark red kidney beans, well drained
1 (15oz.) can small white beans, well drained
salt and pepper to taste

Cook sausage then drain well. Mix all ingredients together and pour into a Pammed baking dish. Bake at 350 for 1 hour.

Serves 12 at 1 fat gram and 554 calories per serving. 14% A, 69% iron, 22% calcium, 258 mg. sodium, 105 g. carb., 36 g. protein, 31 g. fiber

Fruited Wild Rice

I especially love this with pork tenderloin.

1 onion, chopped
1 cup wild and brown rice, mixed
1/4 t. salt
2 -1/2 cups water
1 can (17 oz.) apricot halves, chopped and drained
1/4 cup chopped fresh parsley

Pour 1/4 cup apricot juice in large skillet and saute onion, covered. Add rice and stir until golden. Add salt and water and boil. Reduce heat, cover and simmer 20 minutes. When done, fold in apricots and parsley and heat. Serves 6 at 1 fat gram each.

Herbed Rice

This is a great basic recipe that can be easily jazzed up — add 1 cup sliced, cooked veggies, like mushrooms, celery, peppers, etc. or even a can of drained Mandarin oranges!

2 t. chicken or beef boullion
water according to recipe on box of rice
1/8 t. rosemary
1/4 t. marjoram
1/4 t. thyme
1 t. dried onion
1 cup quick-cooking brown rice

Mix first six ingredients in saucepan and bring to boil. Add rice, reduce heat to low, cover and simmer 15 minutes, or until rice is done.

Serves 4 at 1 fat gram and 160 calories per serving. 37% calcium, 573 mg. sodium, 25 g. carb., 12 g. protein

Judy's Rice Casserole

Always toast nuts when you're watching fat; it brings out the flavor so you can get by with less.

1/2 cup fresh chopped parsley
1 t. honey
1 1/2 t. paprika
1 t. salt
1 1/2 cups basmati rice OR brown rice
1 1/2 cups diced tomatoes or 1 can tomatoes
1 1/2 cups water
1/4 cup raisins
2 T toasted pine nuts

Saute veggies and half the parsley in 1 T. lemon juice and 1T water, covered. When tender, add sugar, paprika, salt and rice. After 1 minute, add tomatoes, water, raisins and bring to simmer. Pour into pammed baking dish, cover and bake at 350 for 1 1/2 hours. Toss with pine nuts and rest of parsley. Serve hot or at room temperature.

Serves 4 to 6 at 2 fat grams and 340 calories per serving. 40% A, 29% C, 14% calcium, 52% iron, 841 mg sodium, 69 g. carb., 9 g. protein

Cornbread Stuffing

I promise this is just as good as my mom's!

2 packages cornbread mix (Jiffy)
1 cup celery, chopped
1 onion, chopped
1 T. garlic
2 T. sage
1 can chicken broth

Prepare cornbread according to directions, omitting
any oil, and using egg whites instead of whole eggs,
and skim milk. When baked, crumble up in bowl.
Saute celery, garlic and onion in 1/8 cup water, covered on stove. Add veggies to cornbread then turn out
in Pammed 9 X 12. Bake at 350 for 30 minutes.
*Serves 10 at 3 fat grams and 111 calories per serving.
506 mg. sodium, 17 g. carb., 3 g. protein*

Gravy
1 can chicken broth, heated
1/4 pan drippings - defatted
1/4 cup flour
1/4 cup cold water

To defat pan drippings, ladle drippings from turkey
pan into heavy measuring cup, the put in freezer for
15-30 minutes. Scrape fat off top, then pour in saucepan. Add broth and heat. In small bowl, mix flour and
water with whisk, then slowly add to broth while
whisking. Let boil and thicken, then season with salt
and pepper. Makes about 2 cups at less than 2 grams
per 1/4 cup.

Nanny's Baked Cheese Grits

My husband begs my mother to make these for every family gathering.

3 cups water
1 cup grits
3 egg whites
2 cups skim milk
1 t. salt
1 cup shredded fat-free cheddar cheese

Boil water and cook grits. Cool slightly, then add eggs and milk and beat until thin. Add remaining ingredients and pour into pammed 2 qt. casserole. Bake at 350 for 45-50 minutes.

Serves 6 - 8 at 0 fat grams and 160 calories. 37 mg. sodium, 573 mg. sodium, 26 g. carb., 12 g. protein

Santa Fe on the Side

This is hearty enough to be a main dish.

2 t. minced garlic
1 large onion, chopped
1 (14.5 oz.) can Mexican, Salsa or stewed tomatoes
1(15-oz.) can black beans, rinsed & drained
1 (5-oz) pkg. saffron or yellow rice (Mahatma)
1/2 cup water
1 cup fat-free cheddar cheese

Spray 2-quart casserole with cooking spray and add garlic and onion. Bake uncovered for about 15 - 20 minutes at 350 then add rest of ingredients except cheese. Mix well. Cover tightly and bake at 350 for 45 minutes or until rice is done. Sprinkle with cheese, cover, and let sit on top of stove until cheese melts. Top with fresh cilantro if desired.

Serves 4 - 6 at 1 fat gram and 318 calories per serv-ing. 17% C, 25 % iron, 570 mg. sodium, 65 g. carb., 14 g. protein

Creamy Rice Casserole

This is a crowd pleaser and is packed with nutrition!

2 1/2 cups cooked brown rice
3 green onions, chopped
1 cup fat-free cottage cheese
1 teaspoon dried dill
1/4 cup fat-free Parmesan cheese
1/2 cup skim milk
1 tablespoon Dijon mustard

Mix all ingredients together and pour in a 2-quart cassrole that has been sprayed with cooking spray. Bake at 350 for 35 minutes.

Serves 6 at 1 fat gram and 366 calories each. 23% C, 17% calcium, 280 mg. sodium, 70 g. carb., 15 g. protein

*Main
Dishes*

Grecian Fried Chicken

I have substituted all kinds of unsweetened cereal for cornflakes when I've been too lazy to make one more trip to the grocery store.

1 cup cornflakes
1 T. Cavender's Greek Seasoning
1/2 cup plain fat-free yogurt
4 boneless, skinless chicken breasts

Put cereal and seasoning in plastic bag. Crush with hammer *gently.* Dip chicken in yogurt, then shake each piece in bag. Place on baking sheet that has been generously sprayed with cooking spray. Spray chicken with spray. Bake at 350 for 45 minutes or until chicken is done.

Serves 4 at 4 fat grams and 147 calories per serving. 1163 g. sodium, 2 g carb., 28 g. protein

Oven Fried Chicken

This is almost as good as greasy fried chicken.

4 boneless, skinless chicken breasts
1 cup plain nonfat yogurt (straight from fridge)
1 cup dried Italian bread crumbs
1 cup all-purpose flour
1 T. garlic powder
1/4 cup fat-free Parmesan cheese
1/2 t. thyme
1/2 t. basil
1/2 t. oregano

Spray cookie sheet heavily with Pam. Put dry ingredients, including Parmesan, in plastic bag and shake well.Soak chicken in big bowl of ice water for 5 minutes, then dip all sides of chicken in yogurt. Place in bag and shake to coat. Spray chicken with Pam and put on baking sheet. Bake on bottom rack in 400 oven for 1 hour.

Serves 4 at 4 fat grams and 396 calories per breast. 17% calcium, 18% iron, 381 sodium, 51 g. carb., 33 g. protein

Farell's Sesame Fried Chicken

A friend of mine called me as soon as she made this so I could put it in the newsletter.

4 boneless,skinless chicken breasts
1 cup cornflakes, crushed
1/4 cup sesame seeds
3/4 t. ginger
1/4 t. salt
1/4 t. paprika
1/2 t. black pepper
1/2 cup fat-free plain yogurt
2 T. honey

MIx cornflakes and next five ingredients and put in ziplock bag. Mix yogurt and honey.Dip chicken in yogurt mixture, then put in bag and roll around til covered in cornflake mix. Spray pan with pam, then put chicken on and spray with spray again. Bake at 400 for 45 minutes.

Serves 4 at 4 fat grams and 260 calories each. 308 mg. sodium, 18 g. carb., 31 g. protein

Chicken Cacci-Currin

Dr. Sam Currin made this up for his family.

12 - 16 chicken tenderloins (you can buy these frozen
at Sam's Wholesale)
1 1/2 cups brown rice
1 large onion, chopped
1 can reduced-fat cream of mushroom soup
1 cup sliced mushrooms
1 can artichoke hearts, drained
1(14 oz) can stewed tomatoes - UN drained)
1/2 cup fresh chopped parsley
3 chicken bouillon cubes
1/2 cup water

Spray large casserole with cooking spray, then layer
rice, chicken, onion, mushrooms, and artichokes in pan.
Mix tomatoes with soup, bouillon cubes and water, and
pour over chicken. Sprinkle with parsley and cover very
tightly and bake at 350 for 45 minutes.

*Serves 4 - 6 at 2 fat grams and 316 calories each. 946
mg. sodium, 45 g. carb., 23 g. protein*

Crock Pot Chicken

This is a wonderful way to have dinner ready when you're not! My husband eats the leftovers on a hamburger bun.

3 boneless, skinless chicken breasts
1 large red onion
1/2 cup soy sauce
1/4 cup white wine
1/2 cup water
1/4 cup honey
3 carrots, sliced
1 zucchini, chopped
1 cup purple cabbage
juice of 1 lemon
1 teaspoon Cavender's Greek Seasoning

Cut up chicken and throw all ingredients in the crock pot. Cook on high for 3-4 hours. Serve over brown rice. Serves 4 at 3 fat grams per serving. If you don't have a crock pot, try this in a covered casserole in a 300 degree oven.

Serves 6 at 2 fat grams and 155 calories each. 1337 mg. sodium, 20 g. carb., 15 g. protein

Coq Au Vin

(I made this for my husband and myself, thinking my kids wouldn't touch it....they gobbled it up!)

4 boneless, skinless chicken breasts
25 - 30 frozen pearl onions
2 cups mushrooms, sliced
1 can beef stock
1 cup dry red wine
1 1/2 T. Dijon mustard
3/4 t. dried thyme
16 baby carrots

Spray heavy dutch oven with cooking spray, and saute chicken and onions, covered, for about 10 minutes, until chicken is browned. Add rest of ingredients and simmer, covered until chicken and carrots are tender. Serve with pasta if desired.

Serves 4 at 4 fat grams and 324 calories each. 400% A, 65% C, 18% calcium, 1357 mg. sodium, 42 g. carb., 33 g. protein

Chicken Pot Pie

Phyllo is intimidating to me, but worth being nervous over because this is so good!

1onion, chopped
3 stalks celery, chopped
1 cup chopped carrots
1 can mixed vegetables, drained
1/4 cup flour
1 can chicken broth
1/2 cup skim milk
2 chicken breasts, cooked
1/4 t. dried thyme
salt & pepper to taste
10 sheets phyllo pastry, thawed.

First, don't panic over the phyllo. Now, spray nonstick skillet with pam and saute onion, celery and carrots, covered. Stir in flour and stir one minute. Slowly add broth and milk, stirring and cooking til thick and bub-bly. Remove from heat and stir in chicken and sea-sonings. Pour in pammed 2-qt. casserole. Keep phyllo covered so it doesn't dry out. Take one sheet and spray it with cooking spray,   then layer over casse-role. Repeat with rest of layers, then either trim phyllo or roll up to edge of casserole. Cut two slits in pastry to let steam escape and spray again with spray. Bake at 350 for 35 minutes then let stand 5 minutes.

Serves 8 at 2 fat grams and 223 calories per serving. 207% A, 18% C, 14% iron, 553 mg. sodium, 34 g. carb., 14 g. protein

Easy Pot Pie

This crust is tougher than a traditional pie crust,
but boy is it easy!

2 cups cut-up chicken or turkey, white meat
1 can reduced-fat cream of chicken soup
8 ounces fat-free sour cream
1 t. tarragon
16 ounces frozen mixed vegetables
1 pkg. won ton wrappers

Mix soup, sour cream and tarragon and add chicken
and vegetables. Spray 2-quart casserole with cooking
spray and line pan with won ton wrappers, covering
bottom and sides and letting wrappers drape up over
sides. Pour chicken mixture in, then cover top with
more won ton wrappers. (We are basically piecing
together a pie crust.) Roll excess wrappers that are
draped over sides in, forming a little ridge like a real
pie crust. Bake at 350 for 45 minutes.

Serves 6 at 2 fat grams and 207 calories each. 86%
A, 14% C, 212 mg. sodium, 18 g. carb., 17 g. protein

Sandra's Chicken Normandy

This is super-easy and is really good. My bunch demolished it.

4 boneless,skinless chicken breasts
1 large Granny Smith apple or any apple
1/4 t. cinnamon
Worcestershire sauce
1/2 cup low-fat Monterey Jack cheese

Spray pyrex pan with cooking spray. Place chicken in dish. Sprinkle each breast with Worcestershire. Cut apple into thin slices and place 4 - 5 on each breast. Sprinkle with cinnamon. Cover with foil and bake at 350 for 45 minutes. When done, grate cheese on each piece, cover again and let sit out of oven until cheese melts.

Serves 4 at 6 fat grams and 186 calories each. 22% calcium, 189 mg. sodium, 5 g. carb., 30 g. protein

NOTE: I serve this with brown rice and a spinach salad (fresh spinach tossed with red onion, a can of drained Mandarin oranges and T. Marzetti's Spinach Salad Dressing)

Al's Stir Fry

This is a favorite of my kids' and a great way to get those veggies down them.

3 chicken breasts, boneless, skinless
3 cups broccoli, cut up
1 red onion, chopped
1 red pepper, chopped
1 cup mushrooms, sliced
1/2 cup shredded carrots
1 cup Stir Fry sauce (Rice Road from Sam's wholesale has no MSG and reduced sodium)

Marinate chicken in sauce.Cut up chicken and saute in sauce. Add onion. When cooked, add rest of ingredients and cook until tender. Serve over brown rice.

Serves 4 at 171 calories and 4 fat grams per serving. 54% C, 1748 mg. sodium, 17 g. carb., 23 g. protein

NOTE: If you're watching sodium, try a reduced-sodium stir-fry sauce or simply mix reduced-sodium soy sauce and a little brown sugar.

Tomato-Sage Chicken

This makes a delicious sauce for dipping bread!

4 boneless, skinless chicken breasts
1 can chicken broth
1 large onion, thinly sliced
2 t. minced garlic
2 cans tomatoes, stewed or plain
3 T. flavored vinegar (herb or wine)
1 T. crushed sage

Spray large casserole with Pam and add all ingredients. Cover and bake at 300 for 2 hours.

Serves 4 at 4 fat grams and 176 calories per serving.
23% C, 697 mg. sodium, 6 g. carb., 31 g. protein

NOTE: Tomatoes are loaded with vitamins C and A, and are at the top of the list of cancer preventers.

Linda's Ranch Chicken

Linda Edwards at WDEF in Chattanooga asked me to reduce the fat in her favorite recipe. She says she can't tell the difference!

1 (10-1/2) oz can REDUCED fat cream of chicken soup
1 can tomatoes w/ chilies (Rotel)
1 large onion, chopped
3 skinless chicken breasts, cooked & cut-up
1 can black beans, drained
4 cups fat-free tortilla chips
2 cups grated fat-free cheddar cheese

Pour soup and tomatoes in saucepan and add onion. Simmer until onion is done. In 9 x 13 pan, layer 1/2 chicken, 1/2 chips, 1/2 beans and 1/2 sauce. Repeat layers. Cover and bake at 350 for 45 minutes. Top with cheese.

Serves 6 at 2 fat grams and 275 calories per serving. 61% calcium, 576 mg. sodium, 25 g. carb., 37 g. protein

Santa Fe Chicken Ole

This is a family favorite. I love it because it's made all in one pot, and there are rarely leftovers to deal with. If you like, add another chicken breast, but it's very satisfying with just two.

2 boneless, skinless chicken breasts
dash Worcestershire
dash lime juice
1 t. minced garlic
1 onion, chopped
1 -14.5 oz. can Mexican or stewed tomatoes
1-15 oz. can black beans, drained
1 -5 oz. pkg. saffron rice (Mahatma)
1/2 cup water
1 cup fat-free cheddar cheese

Spray 2-qt. casserole with cooking spray and put in chicken and onion. Sprinkle with Worcestershire, lime and garlic and bake for 30 minutes at 350 or until chicken is done. Cut up then add rest of ingredients except cheese. Mix, then cover tightly and bake at 350 for 45 minutes or until rice is done. Sprinkle with cheese, cover and let sit until cheese melts. Top with fresh cilantro (in produce section with parsley) if desired.

Serves 4 generously at 2 fat grams and 623 calories each. 18% A, 33% C, 57% calcium, 43% iron, 947 mg. sodium, 101 g. carb., 47 g. protein

Lizzer's Drunken Chicken

This is a real family favorite!

4 boneless, skinless chicken breasts
fat-free cooking spray
1 envelope Lipton's Onion Soup mix
1 cup white wine
1/4 cup water
1/4 t. paprika
1/4 t. pepper

Spray nonstick skillet with cooking spray, and brown chicken on both sides. Add all other ingredients. Cover and let simmer 30 - 40 minutes.

Serves 4 at 4 fat grams and 198 calories per serving. 953 mg. sodium, 6 g. carb., 28 g. protein

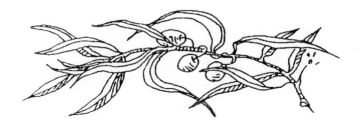

San-San's Tortilla Chicken

This is excellent with the Santa Fe On The Side and a melon salad

4 boneless, skinless chicken breasts
8 ounce block fat-free cream cheese
1 jar salsa
1/2 cup chopped green onions
1/2 cup crushed fat-free or low fat tortilla chips

Put chicken in plastic bag and pound with mallet or hammer. Mix cream cheese, salsa and onions, then spread on chicken. Roll each breast up and secure with toothpick. Spray pan with Pam and put in chicken. Sprinkle with crushed chips, then bake, uncovered at 350 for 35 minutes.

Serves 4 at 4 fat grams and 359 calories per serving. 71% A, 33% C, 22% calcium, 691 mg. sodium, 13 g. carb., 36 g. protein

Natalie's French Onion Chicken

What would I do without my friend Natalie's recipes?

4 boneless, skinless chicken breasts
1 cup white rice
1 cup water
1/2 cup fat-free butter
1 can French Onion soup
1 teaspoon Cavender's Greek seasoning

Spray casserole with cooking spray and add rice and chicken. Pour in water and soup then squeeze butter over all and sprinkle Cavender's over all. Cover well and bake 1 hour at 350.

Serves 4 at 5 fat grams and 332 calories each. 21% A, 17% iron, 1003 mg. sodium, 38 g. carb., 33 g. protein

Caribbean Chicken

This leaves only one dirty dish and it is delicious!

1 onion, chopped
2 t. minced garlic
1 can tomatoes, cut up & undrained
1 can pineapple chunks, undrained
1 T. red wine vinegar
1 T. molasses
3/4 t. ginger
1/2 t. salt
3 boneless, skinless chicken breasts,
    cut up

In dutch oven, add all ingredients. Cover and bake at 350 for 45 minutes. Uncover and broil until toasty. Serve over brown rice.

Serves 4 at 3 fat grams and 257 calories per serving. 488 mg. sodium, 32 g. carb., 28 g. protein

Potato-Crusted Chicken

Everyone in my family is wild for this.

4 boneless, skinless chicken breasts
2 T. Dijon mustard
2 t. minced garlic
1/2 - 3/4 (26-oz.) bag Ore Ida shredded potatoes, thawed
2 T. parmesan cheese

Mix mustard and garlic and rub over chicken. Place chicken in pammed casserole. Spread potatoes over chicken, then sprinkle with parmesan and bake at 425 for 45 minutes or until chicken is done.

Serves 4 at 4 fat grams and 237 calories per serving. 26% C, 208 mg. sodium, 16 g. carb., 23 g. protein

NOTE: My group says the more potatoes the better!

Poulet in a Pot

This is one of the all-time greatest recipes, and it makes the kitchen smell yummy!

4 boneless, skinless chicken breasts
3 potatoes, scrubbed and cut up
2-3 onions, chopped
4-5 carrots, chopped
2 ribs celery
2 cups mushrooms, sliced
1 red or yellow pepper, chopped
1 t. basil
1 bay leaf
1 can chicken broth
1 cup dry white wine

Spray heavy dutch oven with cooking spray, then throw in all ingredients. Cover and bake at 300 for 3 hours. Serve in shallow bowls with lots of sauce for dipping French bread.

Serves 4 at 4 fat grams and 212 calories per serving. 349% A, 72% C, 681 mg. sodium, 19 g. carb., 23 g. protein

Natalie's Fancy Chicken

This is so good and is too easy! It's perfect for company because it's easy on the hostess!

4 boneless, skinless chicken breasts
1/2 cup fat-free plain yogurt
1/2 cup fat-free mayonnaise
2 T. dijon mustard
1 t. Worcestershire sauce
1/4 cup green onions, chopped
1/4 t. garlic salt
1/2 cup fat-free Italian bread crumbs

Mix all ingredients except chicken.Spray pan with Pam, put in chicken and cover with sauce. Bake uncovered at 350 for 45 minutes. Broil for 1-2 minutes when chicken is done.

Serves 4 at 4 fat grams and 225 calories each. 451 mg. sodium, 16 g. carb., 29 g. protein

NOTE: Nat serves this with rice and her own green beans!

Stuffed Chicken Breasts

This is definitely company fare.

6 boneless, skinless chicken breasts
1 (10 oz.) pkg.chopped spinach, thawed and drained
1/2 cup fat-free Parmesan cheese
1 onion, chopped
1/2 cup mushrooms, chopped
1 T. fat-free cottage cheese
1 T. fat-free mayonnaise
1 cup fat-free salad croutons, crushed

In large non-stick skillet, sauté spinach, onions and mushrooms on low heat, covered. When spinach is thawed, add cottage cheese and Parmesan. Pound chicken breasts until flattened. Spread spinach mix-ture on chicken breast, then roll up and secure with wooden toothpick. Place seam side down on Pammed baking dish. Brush chicken with fat-free mayonnaise, then sprinkle evenly with crumbs. Bake at 350 for 1 hour.

Serves 6 at 4 fat grams and 211 calories per serving. 74% A, 24% C, 16% calcium, 409 mg. sodium, 11 g. carb., 33 g. protein

Grilled Italian Chicken

If you can afford to splurge a little, try this with skin-less chicken thighs.

4 boneless, skinless chicken breasts
1/2 cup orange juice
1/4 cup lime juice
1 T. honey
1 T. dijon mustard
2 T. garlic, minced
1 T. oregano

Mix all ingredients in ziplock bag and marinate chicken for 4 hours or overnight. Grill. When done, garnish with orange slices and fresh oregano if desired.

Serves 4 at 4 fat grams each for each breast and 8 fat grams for each skinless thigh. 169 calories per breast, 37% C, 125 mg. sodium, 10 g. carb., 27 g. protein

Grilled Maple Chicken

Believe it or not, this marinade is outstanding on thickly sliced and grilled potatoes!

4 boneless, skinless chicken breasts
2 t. minced garlic
1/2 cup maple syrup
1/2 cup orange juice
1 t. orange zest
1/2 t. thyme
1/2 t. salt
1/8 t. red pepper flakes

In zip lock bag, mix all ingredients except chicken. Add chicken and marinate 4 hours or overnight. Grill. *Serves 4 at 4 fat grams and 248 calories per serving. 29% C, 348 mg. sodium, 30 g. carb., 27 g. protein*

Ellen's Honey-Mustard Marinade
My friend Ellen Moore has called me about four times for this recipe. I figured I'd better include it.

1/2 cup honey
1/4 cup dijon mustard
1 t. curry powder
4 boneless, skinless chicken breasts

Mix all together in zip lock bag and marinate 4 boneless, skinless breasts. Grill or bake.
Serves 4 at 4 fat grams and 261 calories each. 91 mg. sodium, 35 g. carb., 27 g. protein
This is delicious with fat-free cheese grits.

Lemon-Thyme Marinade

*I can't begin to count how many times we've made this.
We absolutely love it.*

4 skinless chicken breasts (4 - oz ea.)
1/2 cup lemon juice
1 t. lemon zest
1/2 cup dijon mustard
1/2 t. thyme
1/4 t. pepper
3/4 t. salt

Mix all ingredients in zip lock bag and marinade chicken
overnight or for 4 hours. Grill over medium -hot coals
until chicken is done.

*Serves 4 at 4 fat grams and 160 calories per serving.
26% C, 853 mg. sodium, 5 g. carb., 28 g. protein*

NOTE: This is excellent with Herbed Pasta.

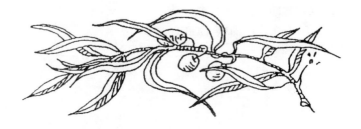

Spicy Chicken with Melon Chutney

This is my husband's very favorite, but it is spicy!

8 boneless, skinless chicken breasts
2 t. salt
1 t. black pepper
1/8 t. cayenne pepper
1 T. dijon mustard
2 t. dried thyme
2 bay leaves, crumbled
1 T. minced garlic
1/2 cup orange juice

Mix all ingredients in zip-lock bag and marinate chicken
4 hours or overnight.
Grill.
Serves 8 at 4 fat grams and 186 calories per serving.
52% A, 72% C, 1194 mg. sodium, 14 g. carb., 27 g.
protein

Melon Chutney

1 mango,peeled and cut up
1/2 cup cantaloupe, chopped
1/4 cup minced purple onion
1 T. lemon juice

Mix all together and chill.

Blackberry Grilled Chicken

Don't let the name scare you; this is delicious!

3/4 cup brown sugar
1 - 8 oz. can tomato sauce
1 - 8 oz. can pineapple tidbits with juice
1/2 cup blackberry jam
1/2 teaspoon dijon mustard
4 -6 boneless, skinless chicken breasts

Spray oblong pan with cooking spray and mix all ingredients, except chicken, in pan. Layer chicken in pan and cook at 350 for 45 minutes, turning chicken once and basting every now and then. This can also be used as a marinade and basting sauce for grilled chicken. *There is no fat in the sauce, and 4 fat grams and 360 calories in each 4-ounce breast. 28% C, 455 mg. sodium, 60 g. carb., 28 g. protein*

NOTE: This is delicious with Baked Cheese Grits and the Buckhead Salad.

ChickaSaw Chicken

I always make extra marinade because I love this sauce!

4 boneless, skinless chicken breasts
1/2 cup minced onion
2 T. brown sugar
2 T. cider vinegar
2 T. dijon mustard
1 t. chili powder
1 t. Worcestershire sauce
1 t. minced garlic
1/2 cup catsup

Mix all ingredients except chicken in zip-lock bag, then pour half of marinade in bowl and reserve. Marinate chicken in bag for 4 hours, then grill. Serve with extra sauce THAT HAS NOT BEEN IN CONTACT WITH RAW CHICKEN.

Serves 4 at 4 fat grams and 237 calories each. 548 mg. sodium, 27 g. carb., 27 g. protein

Grilled Tarragon Chicken

This has a delicate flavor.

1/2 cup fat free mayonnaise
1 T. garlic
1 T. tarragon
1 T. lemon juice
4 boneless, skinless chicken breasts

Mix all ingredients in zip-lock bag and marinate chicken overnight or all afternoon. Grill over medium-hot coals.

Serves 4 at 4 fat grams and 154 calories. 328 mg sodium, 5 g carb., 26 g. protein

NOTE: I love marinades and think they often make the chicken. HOWEVER, you cannot eat any marinade that has been in contact with raw chicken.

Before you add the chicken to any marinade, pour a little extra into a dish, refrigerate it, and serve it with the dinner.

Pearl's Roast Stuffed Pork Tenderloin

If you're ever in Sewanee, TN, you've got to eat at Pearl's. It's wonderful!

1 pkg. (2 lbs.) pork tenderloins, fat trimmed
1/2 cup Major Gray's Mango Chutney (with condiments at grocery)
2 t. basil
2 T. Parmesan cheese
2 t. parsley
1 T. feta cheese
1/4 t. salt
1/4 t. cracked pepper

Split tenderloins lengthwise almost through, but not quite. Place in zip lock bag or cover with Saran wrap and pound with a hammer. Sprinkle salt and pepper on inside of meat, then sprinkle on basil, Parmesan, parsley and feta. Spoon chutney over meat, but don't spread because it will make a mess. Roll tenderloins up lengthwise, and secure with toothpicks. Place seam side down on baking pan and bake at 350 for about 1 hour and 15 minutes until brown.

Serves 6 at less than 5 fat grams and 235 calories per serving. 272 mg. sodium, 11 g. carb., 33 g. protein

Coca-Cola Grilled Pork Tenderloins

This almost tastes like beef!

1 pkg. pork tenderloins (1 1/2 - 2 lbs.)
3/4 cup Coca-Cola
1/4 cup Worcestershire sauce
1 tablespoon apple cider vinegar
2 cloves garlic
1/2 teaspoon red chili pepper
1/2 cup ketchup

Mix all ingredients in a zip lock bag, then reserve 1/2 cup in fridge. Then add tenderloin to bag. Marinate overnight or all afternoon. Grill tenderloin over medium-hot coals with lid down for about 20 minutes. Serve with reserved sauce.

Each 4 oz. serving has 2.5 fat grams and 168 calories. 819 mg. sodium, 8 g. carb., 24 g. protein

Pork Medallions with Apricot Glaze

This makes a beautiful presentation — you can overlap the slices of meat in a circle and drizzle sauce over all. I promise you won't have to worry about leftovers.

1 pkg. pork tenderloins (1 1/2 - 2 lbs.)
1 T. dijon mustard
1 t. dried thyme
1/4 cup sherry
1/4 cup soy sauce
1 t. minced garlic

Apricot Glaze
1-10 oz. jar apricot preserves
1 T. soy sauce
2 T. sherry

Marinate pork in mixture of first five ingredients over-night. Grill and then slice when meat is no longer pink. Mix apricot preserves, soy sauce and sherry and heat until preserves melt. Drizzle over meat.

Serves 6 at 3 fat grams and 143 calories per serving. 495 mg. sodium, 1 g. carb., 24 g. protein

Country Boy Pork Tenderloins

I serve these with apple butter on the side.

2 pork tenderloins (about 1 1/2 to 2 lbs. total)
3/4 cup apple butter
1/2 cup white vinegar
1 1/4 T. Worcestershire sauce
1 T. brandy
1 1/2 t. soy sauce
1 1/2 t. sugar
1/2 t. dry mustard
1/2 t. salt
1/4 t. pepper
1/4 t. paprika
dash Tabasco

Combine marinade ingredients in zip lock bag then marinate pork overnight or all afternoon. Grill.

Serves 5 -6 4 oz. portions at 3 fat grams and 196 calories each. 216 mg. sodium, 15 g. carb., 24 g. protein

Orange Grilled Pork

This is perfect for company because it's easy, delicious and gorgeous.

2/3 cup orange marmalade
4 T. Dijon mustard
1 pork tenderloin, trimmed of fat
3 bunches green onions, sliced

In small saucepan mix marmalade and mustard. Stir over medium heat until marmalade is melted,then pour half into ziplock bag and marinate pork overnight. Grill pork, basting with sauce.When done, slice and arrange on large platter garnished with orange wedges and big bunches of Italian parsley. Just before serving, spray skillet with cooking spray and stir-fry green onions until crisp-tender. Stir in reserved glaze and heat. Serve with pork or pour over platter.

Serves 6 at 4 fat grams and 225 calories per serving. 21% C, 174 mg. sodium, 22 g. carb., 15 g. protein

Lazy Loins

This recipe got its name because we're talking three ingredients and this meat is yummy!

1 package pork tenderloins (NOT ROAST) about 1 1/2 to 2 lbs.
1 T. molasses
1 t. minced garlic
1/4 cup soy sauce

Trim all visible fat from meat. Mix all ingredients in zip lock bag and put tenderloins in to marinate overnight or 4 hours. (I never am organized enough to do this and they still turn out great!) Grill on medium heat until center is no longer pink(20 - 30 minutes).

Every 4-oz. portion is 2.5 fat grams and 147 calories. 472 mg. sodium, 3 g. carb., 24 g. protein

NOTE: Baked sweet potatoes are a must - just prick them and bake for 1 hour at 400. Dollop with brown sugar and fat-free butter!

All Day Barbecue

This is my husband's favorite barbecue recipe; I love to serve this with lots of honey on the side.

2 packages pork tenderloins
1/2 bottle Kraft Hot Barbecue Sauce
3/4 cup apple cider vinegar
1/3 cup molasses
dash Worcestershire
2 tablespoons mustard
juice of 2 lemons
crushed red pepper to taste

Mix all ingredients except meat in large bowl. Marinate tenderloins in about half of sauce all afternoon or overnight. Place over medium coals and baste with sauce fairly constantly. Grill until meat is no longer pink, about 20 - 30 minutes.

Every 4 oz. portion is 2.5 fat grams and 169 calories. 198 mg. sodium, 8 g. carb., 25 g. protein

Jack's Whiskey Q

This makes a quart of sauce, but every time I try to cut back, I regret it. It keeps in the fridge.

1 pkg. pork tenderloins - 1 1/2 to 2 lbs.
1 t. dry mustard
2 cups ketchup
1/2 cup bourbon, or to taste
1/2 cup molasses
1/2 cup cider vinegar
2 T. Worcestershire sauce
2 T. lemon juice
1 T. soy sauce
2 cloves garlic, crushed
1/2 t. pepper
1 T. dried parsley

Spray sauce pan with cooking spray and mix dry mustard and 1/4 cup ketchup. Gradually add rest of ketchup, stirring constantly. Add rest of ingredients and bring to boil, then simmer 10 minutes. Add Tabasco for heat. Marinate pork in zip lock bag with about 1/2 cup of sauce, and use more sauce for basting. When meat is no longer pink, chop up and mix with even more sauce.

Each 4 oz. portion is 2.5 fat grams and 327 calories. 19% A, 1277 sodium, 41 g. carb., 25 g. protein

Honey Roasted Turkey Breast

This makes a wonderful glaze - when the turkey is done, you may want to add a little water to the pan and stir up the glaze.

1 (5-lb.) turkey breast
salt and pepper to taste
1/3 cup honey
3 T. Dijon mustard
1 T. dried rosemary

Pull skin off turkey and season bird with salt and pepper. Mix honey, mustard and rosemary and pour over turkey. Cover loosely with foil and bake at 325 for about 2 hours, basting every 45 minutes or so.

Serves about 12 at 4 fat grams and 186 calories for each 4 ounce serving. 132 mg sodium, 8 g. carb., 32 g. protein

Paul's Early Bird

For years my father has gotten up at the crack of dawn - 9 am in my family- to put this bird in the oven at 250 degrees. It's a wonder none of us ever got food poisioning!

1 (14-pound turkey), thawed
1 orange, 1 apple, 1 onion
2 T. salt
1 T. paprika
1 1/2 T. cayenne pepper
2 T. onion powder
1 T. thyme
1 T. pepper
1 1/2 T. garlic powder
3-5 cloves peeled garlic

Wash turkey and stuff orange, apple and onion in cavity. Mix spices together and rub all over turkey. Loosen skin around neck and stick garlic cloves in. Put bird in large Brown-in-Bag, prick bag with fork, and bake at 325 for 5-6 hours. Serves about 12 with sandwich leftovers.

Breast wth no skin is 4 fat grams and 178 calories for serving about the size of card deck. Dark meat is about 8 grams of fat and 251 calories. Skin adds about 10 grams of fat.

86 mg. sodium for dark meat; 73 mg. sodium for white meat

Turkey Divan

This was my grandmother's recipe...minus the fat!

2 cups cut up turkey breast
2 packages frozen chopped broccoli, thawed and drained
1 onion, chopped
1/2 cup fat-free mayonnaise
1/2 cup fat-free sour cream
1/2 cup low-fat cottage cheese
1 T. lemon juice
salt & pepper to taste
fat-free cheddar cheese

In mixing bowl, mix mayo, sour cream and cottage cheese then add lemon juice. Mix in remaining ingredients, except cheddar, then pour in pammed casserole. Cover and bake at 350 for 40-50 minutes. top with cheese.

Serves 4 at less than 2 fat grams each and 286 calories. 71% A, 139% C, 57% calcium, 2490 mg. sodium, 19 g. carb., 44 g. protein

NOTE: I am bad about using "pammed" as a verb. It simply means to spray your pan with a fat-free cooking spray.

Quickie Croquettes

Believe it or not, my kids love these. I serve them with Potatoes No Gratin.

1-14.7 oz. can salmon, drained
1/2 cup oatmeal, UNCOOKED
1/2 cup skim milk
1 egg white
1 teaspoon dried rosemary

Mix all together and shape into 6 patties. Place on heavily Pammed cookie sheet and bake at 350 for 15 minutes. Flip with spatula and bake 20 more minutes.

Makes 6 at 6 fat grams and 127 calories each. 21% calcium, 454 mg. sodium, 6 g. carb., 15 g. protein

NOTE: Try to eat more fish! Just 2 ounces of fish a week reduces the risk of heart disease substantially. I hate to cook it, so I order salmon, tuna or mackeral (the highest in valuable Omega-3 fatty acids) whenever my husband takes me to out to dinner.

Spinach Quiche

I make extra rice and save leftovers for this!

1 1/2 cups cooked brown rice
2 T. parmesan cheese
1 egg white

1 (10 oz.) pkg frozen spinach
1 cup skim milk
4 egg whites
1 onion, chopped
1/2 cup mushrooms, chopped
1/2 cup fat free parmesan cheese
1 cup fat-free mozzarella cheese

Mix rice, egg white and 2 T. parmesan and spread out in pammed 9" pie pan. Thaw spinach and squeeze out all the water, then mix with remaining ingredients, except mozzarella. Pour into rice crust and bake at 375 for about 1 hour. When done, top with mozzarella and let sit on top of stove until cheese is melted.

Serves 6 at less than 1 fat gram and 444 calories per serving. 119% A, 33% C, 75% calcium, 17% iron, 779 mg. sodium, 71 g. carb., 30 g. protein

NOTE: Studies have shown that spinach can prevent cataracts by protecting the lens of the eye from oxidative damage.

Angie's Red Bean's & Rice

My friend Angie's three boys really love this and as a working mother, she can throw it together in no time!

1 onion, chopped
1 green pepper, chopped
1 clove garlic, minced
1 Louis Rich kielbasa sausage, sliced
1 (14-oz) can Italian tomatoes or stewed tomatoes
2 (14-oz.) cans red beans, drained & rinsed
1/2 t. thyme
1 bay leaf
salt & pepper

"Saute" onion, pepper and garlic in about 1/8 cup of tomato liquid (from can). When translucent, add sausage, cover and cook 8 -10 minutes. Then add rest of ingredients. Cover and simmer for 30 - 45 minutes, stirring every now and then. Serve over rice.

Serves 4 at less than 2 fat grams and 692 calories per serving.13% A, 69% C, 31% calcium, 93% iron, 193 mg. sodium, 126 g. carb., 48 g. protein

NOTE: Beans are right up there with oranges as antioxidants!

Monkey Hips & Rice

I love this nickname for black beans.

1 can chicken broth
1 cup long grain rice
1 large onion, chopped
2 cloves garlic,minced
1 teaspoon olive oil
2 (16-oz) cans black beans, drained and rinsed
1 can crushed tomatoes
2 tablespoons red wine vinegar
1/8 teaspoon cayenne or to taste
3 tablespoons fresh cilantro

Combine chicken broth and rice in saucepan and bring to boil. Reduce heat and cover tightly and simmer for 20 minutes or until rice is done. Meanwhile, in large non-stick skillet cook onion and garlic in oil until onion is soft (about 5 minutes). Add beans, tomatoes, vinegar and cayenne and simmer for 5 minutes. Stir in rice, cilantro and season with salt and pepper to taste. Top with fat-free cheddar cheese or fat-free sour cream if desired.

Serves 6 at less than 3 fat grams and 664 calories per serving. 17% C, 22% calcium, 54% iron, 423 mg. sodium, 122 g. carb., 38 g. protein

Pasta

Creamy Chicken and Pasta Casserole

This makes a wonderful dinner and is good enough for company!

4 boneless, skinless chicken breasts
3 bay leaves
1 chicken bouillon cube
12 oz. box angel hair pasta
juice of 1 lemon
3 stalks celery, chopped
2 large onions, chopped
12 oz. pkg mushrooms, sliced
1 t. garlic, minced
1 T. dried basil
1 t. Worcestershire sauce
salt & pepper to taste
1 can reduced-fat Cream of Mushroom soup
1(8-oz) carton fat-free sour cream
2 cups fat-free cheddar cheese

Boil chicken with bay leaves and bouillon cube. Remove and cut up, reserving water. Boil pasta in reserved water until done. Drain. Meanwhile, spray nonstick skillet with Pam and squirt in lemon and add celery, onions, garlic and mushrooms. Cover and cook until tender. When done, mix soup with sour cream and add seasonings. Mix with pasta, chicken and veggies. Turn out into pammed 9x13 deep casserole, cover and bake at 350 for 45 minutes. Uncover and top with fat-free cheddar cheese and let sit on top of stove until melted.

Serves 8 - 10 at 4 fat grams and 350 calories each. 13% A, 12% C, 799 mg. sodium, 42 g. carb., 29 g. protein

Passionate Latin Pasta

An easy yet romantic dinner for two!

2 cloves garlic
1 large onion, chopped
juice from 2 lemons
2 T. capers
1 1/2 cups sliced fresh mushrooms
1/2 cup sun dried tomatoes, not packed in oil.
3/4 cup dry white wine
1/2 pound cooked and peeled shrimp

Pour about 1/2 cup of boiling water over tomatoes and let sit. Saute garlic and onion in about 2 tablespoons of wine. When onions are cooked, add lemon juice, capers, mushrooms, wine and tomatoes. Cover and cook about 5 minutes. Add more wine if necessary. Add shrimp and cook until shrimp are hot. Serve over pasta and top with parmesan.

Serves 2 generously at less than 3 fat grams and 402 calories per serving. 32% iron, 21% C, 759 mg. sodium, 51 g. carb., 32 g. protein

NOTE: You can make this with raw fresh shrimp — just add to mushroom mixture and stir until shrimp are pink.

Kinda Carbonara

Roasting the vegetables makes all the difference!

1 large onion, sliced in thin rings
2 cloves fresh garlic
8 plum tomatoes, sliced
2 tablespoons Parmesan cheese
2 (10 - oz.) pkg. frozen asparagus
12 oz. angel hair pasta
3 cups fresh spinach
1 teaspoon Cavender's Greek Seasoning, or to taste
3 slices turkey bacon, cooked

Spray cookie sheet with Pam and put tomatoes and onions on. Tuck garlic UNDER tomato, then sprinkle all with parmesan. Broil until cheese is lightly browned.
Boil water in large pot and throw in frozen asparagus (if in pouch, cut out of pouch). Bring water to boil again, then put in pasta and boil 3 - 5 minutes until done. Immediately throw in spinach and the second it's done (less than 1 minute) drain all in colandar. Toss pasta with tomatoes and onions and season with Cavenders..Crumble bacon over top.

Serves 4 at 2 fat grams and 436 calories each. 95% A, 165% C, 35% iron, 543 mg. sodium, 84 g. carb., 21 g. protein

Ravioli Primavera

This is very, very good!

2 T. Naturally Fresh Balsamic Vinaigrette or balsamic vinegar
2 - 3 large portabella mushrooms, sliced
6-8 stalks fresh asparagus
2 large red onions, sliced
1 tomato,sliced
2 cloves garlic
1 (9-oz.) pkg. reduced-fat Contadina ravioli

Saute mushrooms and asparagus in vinaigrette or balsamic vinegar. Place onions and tomato and garlic on pammed cookie sheet and roast at 400 until onion is lightly browned (about 15 minutes). Cook ravioli according to directions and drain, then toss with all vegetables. Sprinkle with parmesan cheese if desired.

Serves 3 generously at 4.5 fat grams and 161 calories per serving. 18% A, 45% C, 735 mg. sodium, 25 g. carb., 9 g. protein

(My husband and I eat this for dinner, then I save the leftovers for my lunch.)

Spinach Calzones

Freeze any leftover sauce. It's delicious over pasta!

16 frozen bread dough rolls, thawed
2 cups fat-free ricotta cheese (15-oz)
1 cup fat-free mozzarella cheese
1 1/2 T. chopped cilantro
1 pkg. chopped spinach, thawed & drained

Let bread rise then roll out each roll to about 3-4 inch diameter.Mix cheeses and cilantro, then put a heaping spoonful of the cheese mixture on one roll. Top with spinach and place another roll on top. Pinch edges together. Repeat with all rolls, then place on pammed baking sheet and bake at 450 for 12 minutes. Serve with tomato sauce. (See next page.) These freeze great, so make tons, freeze on cookie sheets, then store in ziplock bags.

Each calzone has 127 calories and 2 fat grams each. 32% A, 25% calcium, 442 mg. sodium, 15 g. carb., 9 g. protein

Tomato Sauce

If you're really in a pinch, substitute a fat-free sauce like Healthy Choice or Classico--just be sure and check the fat count on the jar.

1/2 cup dry red wine
1 onion, chopped
3 large portabella mushrooms,sliced
2 cloves garlic
2 (14.5 oz.)cans tomatoes
4 T. tomato paste
2 T. basil
2 t. sugar
1 t. salt
pepper to taste

Saute onion, mushrooms and garlic in wine, covered.Add rest of ingredients and simmer 1 hour. Let cool then puree in blender.

This sauce is great, and my picky eaters unknowingly gobble up nutritious portabellas (you can substitute any mushroom). This makes a lot of sauce, but I freeze it and serve on pasta.

Makes 16 calzones at 2 fat grams and 27 calories each. 19% C, 175 mg. sodium, 5 g. carb., 1 g. protein

Sandra's Vegetable Lasagna

This is a reader recipe and is outstanding!

1 cup chopped onion
2 cloves garlic, minced
1 8-oz. pkg. mushrooms, sliced
3-4 zucchini, chopped
1 28-oz can tomatoes, cut up & UNdrained
2 6-oz cans tomato paste
2 t. sugar
2 t. salt
2 t. Italian seasoning or 1 t. basil & 1 t. rosemary
1/4 t. pepper
15-oz. fat-free cottage cheese
1 pkg. frozen chopped spinach, thawed & drained
9 lasagna noodles
2 cups fat free Mozzarella
1/4 cup fat free parmesean

Saute onions, garlic, mushrooms and zucchini in a small amount of water, covered. Then add tomatoes, paste, sugar, salt and spices. Bring to boil, reduce heat and simmer 20 minutes.In bowl, mix cottage cheese and spinach. Put 3 uncooked noodles in pammed 13 x 9 pan. Layer 1/3 of sauce, 1/3 of cottage cheese and 1/3 mozzarella. Repeat. Cover loosely with aluminum foil and bake at 375 for 25 minutes. Uncover and bake 20 more minutes. Let stand 10 minutes.

8 - 10 servings at 1 fat gram and 287 calories per serving. 98% A, 86% C, 55% calcium, 23% rion, 1165 mg. sodium, 44 g. carb., 25 g. protein

Black Bean Lasagna

I know this sounds awful, but it's great! Inspired by Benny's Burritos in NYC.

8 oz. can tomato sauce
1-15 oz.can black beans
1 -14 oz. can stewed tomatoes
9 UNCOOKED lasagna noodles
1 lb. 8-oz. fat-free cottage cheese
1 large onion, chopped
8 oz. carton mushrooms, sliced
6 cups fresh spinach
1 cup fat-free Parmesan
2 cups fat-free mozzarella

Mix tomato sauce, beans and tomatoes in bowl. In non-stick skillet saute onion and mushrooms, covered, in 1/4 cup water. Spray 9 x 13 casserole with Pam, and layer with 3 - 4 noodles (it's fine to break one to piece together) Cover with 1/3 tomato-bean mix, then layer with 1/3 spinach, 1/3 mushroom-onion mixture, then spread with 1/3 cottage cheese. Sprinkle with Parmesan, then repeat layers. Cover tightly with foil and bake at 350 for 1 hour. Uncover and bake 15 minutes, then top with Mozzarella.

Serves 8 at 1 fat gram and 648 calories per serving. 55% A, 40% C, 39% calcium, 36% iron, 665

Red Eggplant Spaghetti

A regular winter dish at our house, this is packed with nutrition.

1 eggplant, peeled and chopped
2 onions, chopped
1 green pepper, chopped
3-4 stalks celery, chopped
1 cup mushrooms, sliced
2 T. garlic, minced
2 cans stewed tomatoes, with juice
1/2 cup red wine (optional)
1 T. sugar
1 small can tomato paste
1 small can tomato sauce
2 bay leaves
2 t. basil
dash lemon pepper

Saute veggies in red wine and about 1/4 cup tomato juice from canned tomatoes. When tender, add remaining ingredients. Serve over pasta with lots of fat-free Parmesan cheese.

Serves 8-10 at 1 fat gram and 292 calories per serving. 25% A, 42% C, 22% iron, 366 mg. sodium, 59 g. carb., 10 g. protein

Denise's Marinara Sauce

Denise loves to add to this; mushrooms, artichokes, red peppers, olives.....

2 t. olive oil
2 onions, chopped
4 cloves garlic, chopped
1 (28-oz.) can tomatoes
1/4 cup fresh basil or 1 T. dried basil
2 t. sugar
sea salt to taste
freshly ground pepper to taste

Saute onions and garlic in olive oil. Then add tomatoes and simmer 15 minutes. Add basil, sugar and seasonings and heat through. Serve over pasta.

Serves 4 - 6 at less than 1 fat gram and 86 calories per serving. 24% A, 57% C, 598 mg. sodium, 14 g. carb., 3 g. protein

NOTE: Tomatoes are rich in an antioxidant called lycopene, which prevents colon, rectal and stomach cancer. Tomato sauce has twice the amount as a whole tomato, so enjoy that spaghetti!

Spaghetti Pie

This is a real family favorite!

8 oz. angel hair pasta, cooked
1/3 cup fat-free Parmesan cheese
3 egg whites
3 zucchini, sliced
1 onion, chopped
1/2 green pepper, chopped
1 cup mushrooms, sliced
1 can stewed tomatoes
1 (8-oz.) can tomato sauce
1 (6-oz.) can tomato paste
1 t. sugar
1 t. oregano
1/2 t. garlic salt
1 cup fat-free cottage cheese
1 cup fat-free mozzarella cheese, shredded

Add Parmesan cheese and egg whites to pasta, then form into crust in pammed 10-inch pie pan. Spray nonstick skillet with Pam, then saute mushrooms, zucchini, onion and pepper. Add tomatoes, tomato sauce, paste, sugar and spices. Spread cottage cheese over crust, then spoon over tomato- veggie mixture. Bake uncovered at 350 for 25 minutes,   then sprinkle on mozzarella and let sit in oven until melted.

Serves 6 at less than 1 fat gram and 285 calories per serving. 30% A, 56% C, 39% calcium, 17% iron, 544 mg. sodium, 45 G. carb., 22 g. protein

Angel Hair with Broccoli

This is as good as it is easy!

1 head fresh broccoli, washed and cut into florets
1 can chicken broth
4 garlic cloves, minced
1 large onion, chopped
1 cup fresh mushrooms, sliced
dash or two of Tabasco sauce
16 ounces angel hair pasta, cooked and drained
1/4 cup freshly grated Parmesan cheese

Bring chicken broth to boil in large saucepan and add
garlic, onion, Tabasco and mushrooms and simmer 10
minutes. Add broccoli and cook about 5 minutes
(don't let it get too done or mushy or dark green).
Serve over pasta and top with Parmesan cheese.
Serves 4 to 6 at 4 fat grams each.

Minute Manicotti

This is fancy enough for company!

1 large onion, chopped
1 (10-oz) pkg. frozen spinach, thawed & drained
1 16 oz carton fat-free cottage cheese
dash nutmeg
1/4 cup parsley
1 t. basil
1 (8-oz. box) manicotti shells, cooked & drained
Spaghetti sauce(Healthy Choice garlic & herb)
11/4 cup fat-free Parmesan
1 cup   fat-free Mozzarella cheese

Put about 1/8 cup water in nonstick skillet and cook
onion, covered, and stirring occassionally, until
transluscent. Mix spinach, cottage cheese, onion,
basil, parsley and nutmeg and stuff mixture in shells.
Place stuffed shells in Pammed casserole, then pour
spaghetti sauce over all.Sprinkle Parmesan cheese
over the top. Bake uncovered for 25 minutes, then
top with Mozzarella. Serves 4 - 5 at 1 fat gram each.

Easy Eggplant Parmesan

A great way to satisfy cravings for Italian
without the fat!

1 eggplant, washed and sliced
1 large onion, chopped
2 egg whites
1/2 cup Parmesan mixed with 1/2 cup flour
1 jar fat-free spaghetti sauce (Healthy Choice garlic &
herb)
1/4 cup fat-free Parmesan cheese
1 cup fat-free mozzarella cheese
cooking spray

Dip eggplant in egg whites, then dredge in flour mix..
Bake on pammed baking sheet with onion at 425
until lightly browned, then flip and brown other side.
Pour thin layer of spaghetti sauce in pammed casserole, layer eggplant and onions, then sprinkle with
Parmesan. Repeat layers. Bake at 350 for 35 - 45
minutes or until bubbly. When baked, top with Mozzarella. Serves 4 at 0 fat grams.

Ellen's Lasagna

This is a real kid pleaser!

1 pound ground chicken (Purdue)
1 large Vidalia onion, chopped
8 lasagna noodles, cooked and drained
1 (26-oz.) jar low-fat spaghetti sauce (Healthy Choice)
1 (16-oz.) carton fat free cottage cheese
1 cup fat free Mozzarella cheese

Cook chicken with onion then drain. In 9x12 greased casserole, layer   four noodles, 1/2 meat, 1/2 spaghetti sauce and 1/2 cottage cheese. Repeat layers and bake at 350 for 30 minutes. When done, top with cheese and let sit on stove until cheese melts.

Serves 6 at 4 fat grams and 465 calories per serving. 29% A, 19% C, 25% calcium, 927, mg. sodium, 40 g. carb., 36 g. protein

NOTE: When buying ground chicken or ground turkey, be sure it says "breast meat only"; otherwise it can contain fat, grizzle, and what have you.

Tequila Shrimp

I could eat this every night!

1/4 cup Knorr's Tequila Lime Marinade (in bottle with marinades at grocery store)
2 large red onions
1 t. minced garlic
2 cups mushrooms, sliced
2 cups (or more) fresh shrimp, peeled & deveined
8 ounces fettucini, cooked and drained

Pour marinade in nonstick skillet and saute onions, covered. Add mushrooms, garlic, then shrimp. Cook until shrimp is pink. Serve over pasta and top with Parmesan.

Serves 4 at 2 fat grams and 324 calories each. 15% C, 24% iron, 336 mg. sodium, 55 g. carb., 20 g. protein

Fettucini Florentine

This is another easy dinner when the pantry is bare!

1 10-oz. pkg. frozen spinach
1 T. lemon juice
1 T. garlic, minced
1 onion, chopped
Fat Free Parmesan
8 oz. fettucini

Spray skillet with Pam and warm spinach with garlic and onion over low heat, covered. When spinach is thawed & onion cooked, add lemon juice. Toss with fettucini and Parmesan.

Serves 2 at 2 fat grams and 300 calories. 147% A, 42% C, 75 mg. sodium, 61 g. carb., 12 g. protein

Pasta in a Panic

This is as easy as it gets and tastes much better than it sounds!

1 large onion, chopped
2 T. white wine
1 jar low-fat spaghetti sauce
1 can albacore tuna, packed in water, drained
12-ounce box pasta spirals, cooked and drained
Parmesan cheese

Saute onion in wine, covering and stirring often, until tender. Add pasta sauce and tuna and heat through. Serve over pasta with lots of Parmesan.

Serves 6 at 1 fat gram per serving and 79 calories. • 26% A, 31% C, 984 mg. sodium • 10 g. carb., 9 g. protein

Herbed Pasta

This is a staple at our house with grilled meats.

8 oz. angel hair pasta
2 bay leaves
1 sprig fresh rosemary (optional)
2 T. dried basil
salt to taste
1/4 cup fat-free Parmesan cheese
1 T. fat-free margarine (Fleischmanns)

Cook pasta with bay leaves and rosemary, then drain.
Toss pasta with remaining ingredients. Serves 4 - 6
at 1 fat gram per serving.

*272 calories • 236 mg. sodium • 48 g. carb., 13 g.
protein*

Stan's Summer Spaghetti

This pasta is light enough for the summer and is delicious!

1 28 oz. can tomatoes, cut up
1 8 oz. can tomato paste
3 T. minced parsley
1 green pepper cut up
8 oz. mushrooms, sliced
1 onion, chopped
1 14-oz can spaghetti sauce
1/4 cup water
salt & pepper to taste
2 t. sugar
2 bay leaves
1 t. Worcestershire sauce

Sautee veggies in water, then add remaining ingredients. Simmer for an hour, stirring occassionally. Serve over pasta with fat-free parmesan cheese.

Serves 8 at 1 fat gram and 107 calories per serving. 38% A, 71% C, 348 mg. sodium, 20 g. carb., 3 g. protein

Roasted Primavera Pasta

If you don't have this dressing, use your favorite fat-free salad dressing (Walden Farm's Sun Dried Tomato Italian is good) or plain balsamic vinegar.

3 zucchini, sliced
2 red onions, cut up
10 - 12 new potatoes, quartered
1 red pepper, cut up
1 T. minced garlic
1/2 t. lemon pepper
1/4 cup Naturally Fresh Balsamic Vinaigrette Salad Dressing

Toss veggies with pepper and dressing and place in pammed roasting pan. Roast at 400 until veggies are tender (about 45 minutes). Toss with sauce below and serve over fettucini.

Sauce
3 T. fat-free Parmesan cheese
2 T. fat-free sour cream
2 T. fat-free yogurt
1 T. lemon juice
1/4 cup white wine
1 T. minced garlic

Mix all together.

Serves 4 at 1 fat gram and 292 calories per serving. 29% A, 166% C, 550 mg. sodium, 60 g. carb, 10 g. protein.

Desserts

German Chocolate Caramel Bars

Ohmygosh these are good!

1 box German chocolate cake mix
1 can FAT-FREE condensed milk
1-12 oz. jar caramel sauce
2 T. reduced-fat chocolate chips

Mix cake mix with condensed milk; batter will be very thick. Press two-thirds of batter into pammed 9x13 pan and bake at 350 for 8 minutes. Take out of oven and pour caramel topping over cake, then sprinkle chocolate chips over all. Crumble remaining cake batter over all and bake at 350 for 15-17 minutes. Makes 24 bars at 2 fat grams each. These are wonderful warm with fat-free frozen yogurt!

Nutritional data not available.

NOTE: 1 packet Equal (1/4 t.) = 2 t. sugar
      6 packs Equal (1-3/4 t.) = 1/4 cup sugar
      12 packs Equal (3-1/2 t.) = 1/2 cup sugar
      24 packs Equal (7 - 14 t.) = 1 cup sugar

Rocky Road Brownies

These are chewy, chocolately and in a word, sinful! Everything chocolate should be, except high in fat!

1 (20-oz) pkg lite brownie mix
1 (5 oz.) can evaporated skim milk
1 (10 oz.) bag miniature marshmallows
1/3 cup reduced fat chocolate chips

Add evaporated milk to brownie mix and pour into pammed 9x12. Bake 23 - 25 minutes. DO NOT OVER-BAKE! Remove from oven and cover with marshmallows and chocolate chips. Broil until marshmallows are golden brown.

Makes 48 brownies at 2 fat grams and 50 calories each. 184 mg. sodium, 202 carb., 6 g. protein

NOTE: After you check with your doctor, walk, walk, walk! Exercise is good for you both physically and mentally.

Well! Oh! Dollies

These are definitely a good substitute for those fat-laden Hello Dollies'!

1 package reduced-fat graham crackers (11 whole)
1 cup frozen coconut, thawed
3/4 cup reduced fat chocolate chips (Ghirardelli)
1 can fat-free condensed milk

Put graham crackers in zip lock bag and gently crush with hammer. Spray 8x8 pan with cooking spray and spread graham crackers in bottom. Sprinkle with chips, add coconut then cover with condensed milk. Bake at 375 for 30 minutes. Makes 24 bars at 2 fat grams each.

Other nutritional data not available.

Lemon Pie Bars

These are just as good as the fattening kind!

2 cups flour
1/2 cup powdered sugar
4 ounces fat-free cream cheese
2 T. fat-free margarine

Mix flour and sugar in large bowl. Cut in cream cheese and margarine until mixture is crumbly. Press into bottom of pammed 9x12 baking pan and bake at 350 for 20 minutes. Pour filling (see below) over hot pastry and bake about 20 - 25 more minutes.

Lemon Filling
5 egg whites
1-1/2 cups sugar
1- 1/2 T. grated lemon rind
1/3 cup flour
1 t. baking powder
1/2 cup lemon juice

Beat egg whites with sugar, then add rest of ingredients., mixing well.

Makes 48 bars at less than 1 fat gram and 56 calories each. 30 mg. sodium, 13 g. carb., 2 g. protein

Caramel Apple Pie

This tastes as good as its name!

8 oz. block FAT FREE cream cheese
1 egg white
1 t. vanilla
3 T. brown sugar
1 T. flour
1 -21 oz. can apple pie filling
1 reduced-fat graham cracker crust (Keebler)
1 - 12 oz. jar caramel topping

Mix cream cheese, egg white, vanilla, brown sugar and flour until smooth. Spread mixture over pie crust. Spread apple pie filling over cream cheese mixture, then drizzle caramel topping over all. (Use about 3/4 of jar — I'm greedy and use it all but my oven is a mess!) Place pie pan on cookie sheet to spare your oven. Bake for 40 - 45 minutes at 375 or until apple layer is bubbly.

Serves 8 at 3 fat grams and 380 calories per serving. 14% A, 12% calcium, 521 mg. sodium, 73 g. carb., 7 g. protein

Chocolate Angel Pie

This one's a splurge if you're strict, but worth it!

1/2 cup sugar
1/4 t. cream of tartar
2 egg whites at room temp
3/4 cup reduced fat chocolate chips
1 t. vanilla
3 t. hot water
2 cups fat-free Cool Whip

Beat egg whites, gradually adding sugar, then tartar. When stiff peaks form, spread in pammed pie pan, forming crust. Bake at   275 for 1 hour. Melt chocolate in mircowave,(careful not to burn) then stir in water.Cool slightly. Fold in vanilla and Cool Whip. Turn into cooled meringue shell and chill. Freeze 2 hours for easy cutting.

Serves 8 at 4 fat grams and 131 calories each. 86 mg. sodium, 23 g. carb., 2 g. protein

Renee's Strawberry Angel

This is really pretty, and really good!

1 prepared angel food cake
1 can fat free condensed milk
8-oz pkg. fat-free cream cheese
1 pint strawberries
1 t. almond extract
1 t. lemon juice
8 oz. FAT FREE Cool Whip

Carefully pinch cake out, leaving sides and center intact. (We're basically stuffing the cake.) Mix cake bits, condensed milk, cream cheese, strawberries, flavorings and stuff back in cake. Ice with Cool Whip and freeze. Garnish with mint leaves and strawberries. Serve frozen.

Serves 8 at 1 fat gram and 383 calories each. 34% C, 15% calcium, 629 mg. sodium, 67 g. carb., 9 g. protein

Crunchy Peach Crisp

You can use any kind of pie filling.

1/2 cup uncooked oatmeal
1 cup brown sugar
1 cup low-fat baking mix (Pioneer)
1/2 cup applesauce (kid's snack -pack)
1/4 t. cinnamon
1 can peach pie filling

Mix the oatmeal, applesauce and baking mix.
(You pretty much need to use your hands.) Pat
1/3 of mix into pie pan that has been sprayed
with Pam.Pour in pie filling and crumble remaining oatmeal mix on top. Bake at 350 for 30
minutes. Serve with fat free vanilla frozen yogurt.
*Serves 6 at 0 fat grams and 208 calories. 15%
iron, 311 mg. sodium,46 g. carb., 3 g. protein*

NOTE: You can use any kind of pie filling; we
like apple, cherry, blueberry.....

Rose's Banana Pudding

Dr. Sam Currin tasted this at his office, found out it was almost fat free, and called me immediately with the recipe!

12-oz. Fat-Free Cool Whip
6-oz. pkg vanilla instant pudding
2 1/2 cups skim milk
1 box reduced-fat vanilla wafers
6 ripe bananas
14 oz. can **fat-free** condensed milk

Prepare pudding using skim milk. Fold in Cool Whip and condensed milk. In large bowl layer cookies on bottom and up sides. Then layer sliced bananas on top and spoon over filling. Repeat layers until bowl is full.

Serves 12 at 2 fat grams and 407 calories per serving. 17% calcium, 314 mg. sodium, 69 g. carb., 5 g. protein

NOTE: Drink skim milk! And give it to your children once they're over age two. You can get used to it if I can. I grew up thinking Half&Half was a beverage!

Tiramisu

I made this on Good Day Atlanta and the response was overwhelming!

2/3 cup sifted powdered sugar
8 oz. fat-free cream cheese, softened
1 1/2 cups fat free whipped topping, thawed
1/2 cup sugar
1/4 cup water
3 egg whites
1/2 cup brewed coffee
1 angel food cake
1/2 t. unsweetened cocoa

Slice angel food cake into slices and place on cookie sheet. Broil until golden brown, then layer half in serving dish. Drizzle half of coffee over cake. Beat powdered sugar with cream cheese until blended, then gently fold in 1 cup whipped topping.
Combine 1/2 cup sugar, water and egg whites in saucepan over low heat, and beat with mixer until peaks form. Gently stir 1/4 egg white mixture into cheese mixture, then fold in rest of egg white into cheese. Spread half of cheese mixture over toasted angel food and repeat process. Sprinkle with cocoa. (Freeze two hours before serving for easy cutting.)

Serves 8 at 1 fat gram and 340 calories per serving. 15% calcium, 570 mg. sodium, 71 g. carb., 10 g. protein

Mama's Bread Pudding

This is a great way to use leftover French bread!

1/2 loaf French bread, cut into cubes
2 cups skim milk
3 egg whites, beaten
3/4 cup sugar
1 T vanilla
1/2 cup raisins
2 T. applesauce

Mix milk, egg whites, sugar, vanilla raisins and applesauce. Add bread and mix until all bread cubes are coated. Pour mixture into pammed 2 quart casserole and bake at 350 for 40 minutes. Serve with fat-free vanilla frozen yogurt and store-bought caramel sauce if desired.

Serves 6 - 8 at 0 fat grams and 605 calories, 28% calcium, 28% iron, 920 mg. sodium, 120 g. carb., 18 g. protein

Lemon Trifle

My dad found this recipe.

1 angel food cake, cut into cubes
1 can fat-free condensed milk
2 teaspoon grated lemon rind
1/3 cup lemon juice
1-8 oz. cup fat free lemon yogurt
1 - 8 oz. tub fat-free whipped topping
1 cup strawberries, sliced
1 cup fresh blueberries
1 kiwi, peeled and sliced

Mix condensed milk, lemon rind, lemon juice and yogurt. Fold in whipped topping. Place 1/3 of cake cubes in bottom of 4-quart glass bowl. Top with 1/3 of lemon mixture, then layer 1/3 of the fruit. Repeat layers until finished. Cover and chill.(Any fruit or combo of fruit will do.)

Serves 8 - 10 at 2 fat grams. Other nutritional data not available.

Denise's Forgotten Torte

This is my friend's favorite birthday dessert, and it is fat free as well as delicious and gorgeous!

6 egg whites, at room temperature
1/4 t. salt
1/2 t. cream of tartar
1 1 /2 cups sugar
1 t. vanilla
1/8 t. almond extract
1 cup strawberries, sliced
1 cup blueberries
1 cup Kiwi, sliced

Preheat oven to 425. Beat egg whites with salt and tartar. When peaks form, add sugar, one tablespoon at a time. Add vanilla and almond extract. Pour into pammed tube pan, and turn oven OFF. Leave overnight, then carefully take out of pan. Cover with fruit. (Any combo will do.)

Serves 6-8 with 0 fat grams and 240 calories per serving. 48% C, 147mg. sodium, 56 g. carb., 4 g. protein

Note: When you're beating egg whites, everything must be spotless or they won't peak ... the bowl and beaters... don't worry, not the house.

Luscious Lemon Cheesecake

Woman's World Magazine chose this cheescake out of all my recipes to put on their cover.

3/4 cup reduced fat graham crackers, crushed
5 (8-oz.) pkgs. fat-free cream cheese
1- 2/3 cups sugar
9 egg whites
1 t. grated lemon rind
1/4 cup lemon juice
1 1/2 t. vanilla
1/8 t. salt

Spray bottom and sides of 10" springform pan with cooking spray 3 times. Place graham cracker crumbs in bottom of pan and tilt until bottom and sides are coated. Chill. Beat cream cheese until creamy, gradually adding sugar. Add egg whites one at a time, then stir in remaining ingredients. Bake at 300 for 1 hour and 15 minutes. Garnish with fresh mint leaves and lemon twists.

Serves 10 at less than 1 fat gram and 293 calories per serving. 34% A, 35% calcium, 733 mg. sodium, 46 g. carb., 21 g. protein

Chocolate Cheesecake

This has been at many of our family gatherings and it is delicious!

1 box fat-free chocolate-filled cookies (Snackwell Devil's Food)
2 pounds fat-free cream cheese, softened
2 cups sugar
5 egg whites
2 cups fat-free sour cream
3 T. Hershey's syrup
3 T. powdered cocoa
2 t. vanilla

Put cookies in food processor or blender and whirl until crumbled. Press cookies in pammed springform pan, forming crust on bottom. Put in refrigerator to chill. Beat cream cheese until fluffy, then add sugar. Add egg whites one at a time, beating well after each one. Then blend in sour cream and remaining ingredients. Pour mixture into chilled crust and bake at 350 for 1 hour and 10 minutes. Garnish with fresh strawberries if desired.

Serves 12 at less than 1 fat gram per serving. Other nutritional data not available.

Betty's Coconut Cake

This is easy and delicious!

1-13 oz. fat-free pound cake (Entenmann's)
8 oz. fat-free sour cream (Guilt Free)
2 cups sugar
8 oz. shredded coconut, thawed if frozen

With serrated knife, split cake into 3 layers. Start with a knife cut, then take dental floss and pull all the way through. (Betty does four layers but even two make me nervous.)
Mix sour cream, sugar and coconut. Ice top of bottom layer, then layer cake on top. Ice top and continue layering and icing until this specatular dessert is finished!

Keep refrigerated. If you have extra icing, save it and use it for extra topping.

Serves 8 at 4 fat grams and 272 calories. 39 mg.sodium, 57 g. carb., 2 g. protein.

Dutch Apple Coffee Cake

*I made this for the school's bake sale and
my son bought it!*

1 1/2 cups flour
1/2 cup brown sugar
1 t. baking soda
1/4 t. ground cloves
1/2 t. ground cinnamon
1/3 cup apple butter
2/3 cup fat-free buttermilk
1 egg white
1 can apple pie filling
1 T. brown sugar
1 T. oatmeal, NOT cooked
1 T. fat-free butter

Mix 1 T. each brown sugar, oatmeal and butter for
topping and set aside. Mix flour, brown sugar, soda
and spices, then add apple butter, buttermilk and egg
white. Fold in pie filling. Pour in 8" pammed cake pan
and sprinkle with topping. Bake at 325 for 30 minutes.

*Serves 8 at less than 1 fat gram and 226 calories per
serving. 222 mg. sodium, 53 g. carb., 4 g. protein*

Fudge Gooey Cake

This is one of my most requested recipes!

1 cup flour
2 t. baking powder
1/4 t. salt
3/4 cup sugar
1/4 cup cocoa powder & 1 1/2T. cocoa, divided
1/2 cup skim milk
1 t. vanilla
3/4 cup brown sugar
1 3/4 cups hot water

Mix flour, baking powder, salt sugar and 1 1/2 T. cocoa. Add milk and vanilla and spread in pammed 9" pan. Mix brown sugar with 1/4 cup cocoa and sprinkle over top. Pour water over and DO NOT STIR. Bake 40 - 45 minutes at 350.

Serves 4 with 0 fat grams and 386 calories per serving. 25% calcium, 17% iron, 343 mg. sodium, 92 g. carb., 5 g. protein.

Hawaiian Cake

This is simply luscious and you won't believe it's so low fat!

1 box reduced-fat yellow cake mix
6 egg whites
1 can Mandarin oranges, NOT drained

Mix above ingredients well and pour into two pammed round cake pans. Bake at 350 for 25 minutes. Let cool, then ice.

Icing
1(8-oz) tub Lite Cool Whip
1 (12-oz.) can crushed pineapple
1 5-oz. box vanilla instant pudding
2 tablespoons lemon juice

Do not drain pineapple. Mix all icing ingredients together with mixer until pudding sets and icing is thick enough to ice a cake. Ice the cake!

Serves 12 at less than 4 fat grams and 328 calories per serving. 393 mg. sodium, 45 g. carb., 4 g. protein.

Nanny's Fruited Spice Cake

My mother-in-law brought this over one night and I didn't let her leave until she gave up the recipe!

1 (18.5 oz.) box spice cake mix
1 (4 oz.) jar prune baby food
5 egg whites
1/8 t. EACH salt, ginger & cinnamon
1 (20-oz.) can crushed pineapple
1 cup brown sugar

Mix cake mix with salt, cinnamon and ginger, then add prunes. Add egg whites one at a time. Pour into two pammed round cake pans. Mix pineapple and brown sugar, then pour pineapple mixture over each pan of spice cake batter. Bake at 350 for about 35- 40 minutes. When done, turn each upside down on serving platter!

Serves 12 at 4 fat grams and 254 calories each. 314 mg. sodium sodium, 50 g. carb., 4 g. protein

Sis's Boiled Custard

My sister created this low-fat version of my grandmother's traditional holiday recipe.

8 egg whites
1 quart skim milk
1 cup sugar
1 T. corn starch
pinch salt
vanilla to taste

Mix sugar and cornstarch, then add egg whites one at a time and place in double boiler. Add milk gradually. Cook and stir until mixture coats a spoon (Get a book or the phone - just stay put!) Add vanilla and salt. Serve sprinkled with nutmeg.

Serves about 8 at less than 1 fat gram and 160 calories per serving. 15% calcium, 152 sodium, 32 g. carb., 8 g. protein

Holiday Spice Cake

This is a rich, dense and delicious cake!

2 cups sugar
2 cups cold water
1 cup raisins
1 T. butter
1 T. applesauce
3 cups flour
pinch salt
1 t. baking soda
1 t. ground cloves
1 t. nutmeg
1 t. cinnamon

In saucepan, combine raisins, water, butter, sugar and applesauce. Bring to boil, then simmer ten minutes. Refrigerate 12 hours. Sift remaining ingredients, then add to raisin mixture. Pour in greased cake pan and bake at 325 for one hour.

Serves 10 at less than 1 fat gram and 347 calories per serving. 12% iron, 409 mg. sodium, 80 g. carb., 4 g. protein

NOTE: This is delicious with Sis's Boiled Custard!

Martha's Carrot Cake

Carrot cake on a low-fat diet? Try it. You won't believe it!

4 cups grated carrots
2 cups sugar
1 can (8-oz. crushed pineapple)
1 cup Prune Puree (follows)
4 large egg whites
2 t. vanilla
2 cups flour
2 t. soda
2 t. cinnamon
1/2 t. salt

Mix carrots, sugar, pineapple, prune puree, egg whites and vanilla. In another bowl mix dry ingredients, then mix together. Bake in pammed 9x13 at 375 for 45 minutes.

Prune Puree
Mix 1 1/3 cups (8 oz.) pitted prunes and 6 T. water in blender. Puree. Makes 1 cup.

Serves 10 at 2 fat grams and 214 calories per serving. 300% A, 257 mg. sodium, 51 g. carb., 4 g. protein

Miscellaneous

Saturday French Toast

My family loves weekends when we're not rushing off to sports events and I have time to make this.

3 whole wheat sub rolls
2 egg whites
1 cup skim milk
1 t. cinnamon

Mix egg whites, milk and cinnamon in shallow bowl. Slice sub rolls on diagonal into 1/2 inch slices and dip each one in milk mixture. Spray griddle with cooking spray and, when hot, place bread on griddle. Let cook a few minutes, then flip.

Serves about 4 at 2 fat grams and 185 calories each. 391 mg. sodium

NOTE: You can use any kind of bread; leftover French bread is great sliced, as is regular sliced bread.

Blueberry-Banana Pancakes

These vanish faster than I can make them.

1 ripe banana
8 oz. carton fat-free blueberry yogurt
1/2 cup skim milk
2 egg whites
1 cup plain flour
1 t. baking powder
1/2 t. baking soda

Mash banana and mix with yogurt, milk and egg whites. Sift dry ingredients together and add to banana mixture. Drop by tablespoons onto pammed griddle. When bubbly at edges, flip.

Makes about 14 (4") pancakes at less than 1 fat gram and 85 calories per serving. 108 mg. sodium

Tasty Bran Muffins

This was the very first recipe for fat-free muffins that I didn't throw out. And they are just as moist and tasty as they can be!

2 egg whites
2 T. fat-free margarine (Fleischmanns)
2 T. honey
3/4 cup fat-free buttermilk
1/4 cup whole wheat flour
1/3 cup flour
3/4 cup brown sugar
1 1/2 cups all-bran cereal
1/4 t. salt
1/4 t. baking soda
1/4 t. cinnamon
1/2 cup fruit cocktail

In large bowl, mix egg, margarine, cereal, honey, buttermilk and fruit with beaters. Add remaining ingredients and fold in. Spoon into "pammed" muffin cups and bake at 400 for 15 minutes or until center bounces back.
Makes 12 muffins at less than 2 fat grams and 106 calories each. 151 mg. sodium

Heart Healthy Biscuits

These are surprisingly delicious! My husband loves them with a Healthy Choice sausage inside!

1 T. Canola Oil
1/2 cup fat-free buttermilk
1 cup White Lily self-rising flour

Mix oil and buttermilk first, blending well; immediately add flour. You may have to add more buttermilk to make a soft dough. Turn out on a floured surface and knead until you can handle it. Roll out and cut out biscuits. Place on pammed baking sheet and bake at 400 for about 10 minutes. This makes 4 biscuits and can be increased as needed. Also, you can add 1 T. sugar and make straw-berry short cake biscuits!

Makes 4 at 3.5 fat grams and 153 calories each. 429 mg. sodium.

(I omit the oil totally and they are really good!)

Creamy Pimiento Cheese Spread

This gets raves all around!

2 1/2 cups (10-oz) shredded sharp fat-free cheddar
cheese
1(12-oz.) container fat-free cottage cheese
1/4 cup fat-free mayonnaise
1/8 t. white pepper
4 drops hot sauce
1 (4-oz.) jar diced pimiento, NOT drained

Put first five ingredients in food processor and process
until smooth. Add pimiento and pulse 4-5 times.

*Makes 3 1/2 cups at 0 fat grams and 445 calories per
serving. 258 mg. sodium*

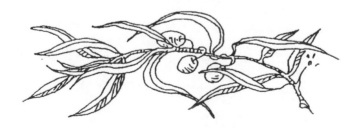

Boyer's Barbecue Sauce for a Bunch

This marinade is one of my all-time favorites. I grill it with the skin on and try my hardest to eat only the meat.

1 quart cider vinegar
12-oz. Fleischmann's Fat Free squeeze butter
1/3 cup salt
1 t. pepper
1 tablespoon chili powder
1/2 - 6 oz. jar mustard
1/2 - 5.oz. jar horseradish
1/2 - 10 oz. bottle Worcestershire sauce
juice of 1 lemon
12 pounds of chicken halves

Mix all ingredients except chicken and simmer in saucepan for15 minutes.Marinate chicken and baste heavily with this during the entire time of grilling.

Makes enough for 12 lbs. of chicken with 4 fat grams per breast, 8 fat grams per thigh and an additional 8 grams of fat for the skin on each piece. 84 mg. sodium in sauce.

Mammy's Cranberry Salad

I can't imagine a holiday dinner without this.

2 packages lemon Jello
1 small can crushed pineapple, drained and JUICE
SAVED
2 cups chopped celery
2 cups chopped apples
1 1/2 cups chopped cranberries
1/2 cup lemon juice
1 1/2 T. grated orange peel

Add enough water to pineapple juice to make 1 1/2
cups liquid. Bring to boil, then pour in Jello. Stir until
dissolved, then add remaining ingredients. Pour into
pan that has been sprayed with cooking spray, then
refrigerate until set. Serves 12 at 0 fat grams.
(If you want to splurge, add 1/2 c. chopped pecans.)

Hallie Q.'s Plantation Tea

My kids choose this over soft drinks!

2 family-sized tea bags
1 (10-oz.) can orange juice
1 1/2 cups pineapple juice
3 T. lemon juice
1 1/2 cups sugar
fresh mint

Put tea bags in about 3/4 gallon of hot water. Let steep to desired strength (10 minutes). Add rest of ingredients and mix well. Makes about 1 gallon with 0 fat grams, 53 calories per glass and lots of vitamins.

Pesto

This is as good as the fat-packed variety!

1/2 cup chopped parsley
1/3 cup Grey Poupon mustard
1/2 cup fat-free Parmesan cheese
2 t. dried basil
2 t. garlic, minced

Mix all ingredients together in blender. Spread on toasted French bread that's been sliced on the diagonal, or spread fat-free wheat crackers with fat-free cream cheese, then top with pesto. Serves 8 at 0 fat grams.

Tarragon Mayonnaise

This is terrific on a turkey sandwich.

1/2 cup low-fat Hellmans' mayonnaise
2 teaspoons dried tarragon

Mix together and let sit for an hour or overnight in the fridge. Makes 1/2 cup.

Susan's Brandied Cranberries

This is delicious and elegant.

1 cup ruby port wine or sherry
1 cup sugar
12 ounces fresh cranberries

Mix all ingredients in a medium saucepan and bring to boil, stirring occasionally. Lower heat and cook until mixture turns syrupy, about 20 minutes. Let cool to room temperature and serve. This can be made ahead of time and refrigerated.

Clark's Cranberry Relish

This is easy beyond belief, and a holiday must!

12-oz. bag fresh cranberries, washed and sorted
1 cup sugar
1 seedless navel orange, unpeeled and quartered

Process all ingredients in food processor until crumbly (careful not to puree it) and serve.

INDEX

APPETIZERS

Bueno Bites	14
Joanie's Sausage Dip	14
Manly Tex Mex	15
Fiery Bean Dip	16
Pure Texas	16
Sherried Cream Cheese with Chutney	17
Hummus	18
Party Pizzas	19
Greek Pastries	20
Baked Artichoke Dip	20
Chicken Fingers	20
Dennie's Corn Relish	22
Summer Salsa	22

SALADS

Buckhead Spinach Salad	24
Broccoli Red Pepper Salad	25
Broccoli Slaw	25
Potato Salad	26
Summer Corn Salad	27
Creamy Broccoli Salad	28
Mandarin Black Bean Salad	29
Creamy Cole Slaw	30
All Night Cole Slaw	31
Betty's Pasta Salad	32
More Ellen Moore Pasta Salad	33
Tisho's Roasted Pepper Pasta Salad	34
Black Bean & Chicken Salad	35
Summer Chicken Salad	36
Chicken Waldorf Salad	37
Tropical Chicken Salad	38
Carrot-Raisin Salad	39
Black Bean & Corn Salad	39
Sally's Tuna Salad	40

SOUPS

Herb-Barley Soup   42
French Onion Soup   43
Cuban Black Bean Soup   44
Clara's Cabbage Soup   45
Mother's Bean Soup   46
Minnesota Minestrone   47
Katie's Black Bean Soup   48
Ice Storm Chill   49
White Chili   50
Cowboy Corn Chowder   51
Tarragon Chicken Soup   52
Marty's Spinach Soup   53
Totally Tortilla Soup   54
Tina's Gazpacho   55
White Bean & Sausage Soup   56

VEGETABLES

Bab's Squash Casserole   58
Creamy Cheesy Squash   59
Cheesy Spinach-Artichoke Casserole   60
Andrea's Cheesy Broccoli   61
Cheesy Tomato Pie   62
Migrit's Corn Pudding   63
Jan's Corn Pudding   63
Nat's Green Beans   63
Very Vidalia Casserole   65
Spicy Zucchini   67
Zucchini Boats   68
Spring Veggies   69
Roasted-Tomato Mashed Potatoes   70
Garlic Mashed Potatoes   71
Buttermilk Mashed Potatoes   72
Potatoes No Gratin   73
Hash Brown Potatoes   74
Ratatouille-Topped Potatoes   75

Three-Cheese Stuffed Potatoes 76
Loaded Baked Potatoes 77
Sweet Potato Boats 78
Tuscanny White Beans 79
Curt's Hoppin' John 80
Susan's Black Baked Beans 81
Bacon-Baked Beans 82
Best Baked Beans 83
Fruited Wild Rice 84
Herbed Rice 85
Judy's Rice Casserole 86
Cornbread Stuffing 87
Gravy 87
Nanny's Baked Cheese Grits 88
Santa Fe on the Side 89
Creamy Rice Casserole 90

MAIN DISHES

Grecian Fried Chicken 92
Oven Fried Chicken 93
Farell's Sesame Fried Chicken 94
Chicken Cacci-Currin 95
Crock Pot Chicken 96
Coq Au Vin 97
Chicken Pot Pie 98
Easy Pot Pie 99
Chicken Normandy 100
Al's Stir Fry 101
Tomato Sage Chicken 102
Linda's Ranch Chicken 103
Santa Fe Chicken Ole 104
Lizzer's Drunken Chicken 105
San-San's Tortilla Chicken 106
Natalie's French Onion Chicken 107
Carribean Chicken 108
Potato Crusted Chicken 109

Poulet in a Pot   110
Natalie's Fancy Chicken   111
Stuffed Chicken Breasts   112
Grilled Italian Chicken   113
Grilled Maple Chicken   114
Ellen's Honey Mustard   114
Lemon-Thyme Chicken   115
Spicy Chicken with Melon Chutney   116
Blackberry Grilled Chicken   117
Chick A Saw Chicken   118
Grilled Tarragon Chicken   119
Pearl's Roast Stuffed Tenderloin   120
Coca-Cola Grilled Tenderloin   121
Pork Mendallions with Apricot Glaze   122
Country Boy Pork Tenderloins   123
Orange Grilled Pork   124
Lazy Loins   125
All-Day Barbecue   126
Jack's Whiskey Q   127
Honey Roasted Turkey Breast   128
Paul's Early Bird   129
Turkey Divan   130
Quickie Croquettes   131
Spinach Quiche   132
Angies Red Beans & Rice   133
Monkey Hips & Rice   134

PASTA

Creamy Chicken & Pasta Casserole   136
Passionate Latin Pasta   137
Kinda Carbonara   138
Ravioli Primavera   139
Spinach Calzones with Tomato Sauce   140
Sandra's Vegetaable Lasagna   142
Black Bean Lasagna   143
Red Eggpplant Spaghetti   144
Denise's Marinara Sauce   145

Spaghetti Pie   146
Angel Hair with Broccoli   147
Minute Manicotti   148
Easy Eggplant Parmesan   149
Ellen's Lasagna   150
Tequila Shrimp   151
Fettucini Florentine   152
Pasta in a Panic   153
Herbed Pasta   154
Stan's Summer Spaghetti   155
Roasted Primavera Pasta   156

DESSERTS

German Chocolate Caramel Bars   158
Rocky Road Brownies   159
Well! Oh! Dollies   160
Lemon Pie Bars   161
Caramel Apple Pie   162
Chocolate Angel Pie   163
Renee's Strawberry Angel   164
Crunchy Peach Crisp   165
Rose's Banana Pudding   166
Tiramisu   167
Mama's Bread Pudding   168
Lemon Trifle   169
Denise's Forgotten Torte   170
Luscious Lemon Cheesecake   171
Chocolate Cheesecake   172
Coconut Cake   173
Dutch Apple Coffeecake   174
Chocolate Fudge Goody Cake   175
Hawaiian Cake   176
Nanny's Fruited Spice Cake   177
Sis's Boiled Custard   178
Holiday Spice Cake   179
Martha's Carrot Cake   180

MISCELLANEOUS

Saturday French Toast   182
Blueberry-Banana Pancakes   183
Tasty Bran Muffins   184
Banana Bran Muffins   185
Elise's Heart Healthy Biscuits   186
Creamy Pimiento Cheese   187
Boyer's Barbecue Sauce   188
Mammy's Cranberry Salad   189
Hallie Q.'s Plantation Tea   190
Pesto   191
Tarragon Mayonnaise   191
Susan's Brandied Cranberries   192
Cranberry Relish   192

To order **The Gorgeless Gourmet Cookbook**, send $14.95 (GA residents add $.75 sales tax) plus $2 shipping (total $16.95) to:

The Gorgeless Gourmet Cookbook
Box 366
Lookout Mountain, TN, 37350.

While you're at it, you might want to order the **Gorgeless Gourmet Newsletter,** a monthly newsletter of easy, low-fat recipes, reviews of new fat-free products and newsworthy tidbits on the fat-free scene. Send $15 (GA residents add $.75 sales tax) to above address and indicate **Newsletter** please.

If you'd like to send the cookbook as a gift, the **Gorgeless Gourmet Cookbook** will be tied with a colorful ribbon and sent with a card with your name on it. You can also send the newsletter as a gift and there is no extra charge for either. Simply print the recipients name and address and send $16.95 for the cookbook or $15 for the newsletter to the above address.